EASY PIANO

BROADWAY'S BEST
COLLECTION

50 SELECTIONS FROM FAVO...

D1430581

Copyright © MMVIII by Alfred Publishing Co., Inc.
All rights reserved.   Printed in USA.

ISBN-10: 0-7390-5779-0
ISBN-13: 978-0-7390-5779-7

42nd Street

Anything Goes

Camelot

The Fantasticks

Gypsy

Mamma Mia!

My Fair Lady

Porgy and Bess®

Ragtime

The Secret Garden

Seussical

Sweeney Todd

42nd Street

42nd Street debuted on Broadway in 1980 at the Winter Garden Theatre in New York City. It subsequently moved to the Majestic Theater and St. James Theater before completing its run of 3,486 performances. After 11 curtain calls on a triumphant opening night, producer David Merrick appeared onstage to announce that the show's director and choreographer, Gower Champion, had died of cancer just hours before the performance. Since this tragedy was news to everyone, including the cast and crew, the dramatic announcement made headlines and garnered an enormous amount of publicity for the new show.

42nd Street is a musical about musicals. Based on the Bradford Ropes novel and the subsequent 1933 motion picture adaptation, the show tells the story of Broadway director Julian Marsh and his efforts to stage an elaborate musical extravaganza at the height of the Great Depression. A talented young chorus girl, Peggy Sawyer, wants to try out for Marsh's new musical, *Pretty Lady*; however, she arrives late and misses the auditions. The star of the musical, Dorothy Brock, is well past her prime, but is cast in the leading role since she's married to the man who is financing the show.

As fate would have it, Dorothy breaks her ankle right before the premiere, which threatens to close the show. This turn of events forces the director to cast young Peggy in Dorothy's place. Peggy learns the part in two days, with help from a cooperative Dorothy. The show is a huge success and is sure to make Peggy a big star. Despite becoming an overnight sensation, Peggy declines her invitation to the fancy opening-night party and attends the chorus party instead.

The original production of *42nd Street* starred Jerry Orbach as Julian Marsh, Tammy Grimes as Dorothy Brock, and Wanda Richert as Peggy Sawyer. It won Tony® Awards for Best Musical and Best Choreography. The show was produced in London in 1984, and won the Olivier Award for Best Musical. It was revived on Broadway in 2001 at the Ford Center for the Performing Arts, and earned Tony Awards for Best Revival and Best Actress in a Musical (Christine Ebersole).

A classic celebration of Broadway, *42nd Street* is filled with spectacular dance routines and memorable music.

Anything Goes

Anything Goes debuted on Broadway in 1934 at the Alvin Theater in New York City and had an initial run of 420 performances—a record at the time.

The main action takes place on board the S.S. American, a luxury cruise ship heading for England. Love-sick Billy Crocker, a young Wall Street broker, stows away on the ship in an effort to pursue his former flame, Hope Harcourt. Hope is engaged to a British nobleman, Lord Evelyn Oakleigh, but Billy wants to win her back despite the dismay of Hope's mother, Evangeline Harcourt. Billy enlists his friend, Reno Sweeney, a larger-than-life nightclub singer (played by Ethel Merman in the original production), to help win Hope back. Two gangsters agree to help Billy as well, provided Billy doesn't give away their identity. A variety of eyebrow-raising situations ensue, but, in the end, Billy and Hope are reunited.

Cole Porter's score for *Anything Goes* was an instant hit on Broadway, and many of the songs—"Anything Goes," "Easy to Love," "I Get a Kick Out of You," "It's De-Lovely" and "You're the Top," to name a few—made their way onto the pop charts and are now considered standards. Over 50 years after its debut, *Anything Goes* won the Tony Award for Best Revival, solidifying its place as a landmark American musical.

Camelot

Camelot, based on T. H. White's novel *The Once and Future King*, was the last collaboration of the celebrated team of Lerner and Loewe. The original production was directed by Moss Hart and opened on December 3, 1960, at the Majestic Theater. The show ran for 873 performances before closing on January 5, 1963.

Set in the time of Arthurian England, the story begins with a young King Arthur, nervous about his impending arranged marriage to the maid Guenevere, being counseled by his tutor Merlyn. In the forest, Arthur runs into Guenevere, who also has been fretting over her future as Queen. They find themselves smitten with each other and excited by the possibilities of royal life in Camelot. Years later, the knight Lancelot arrives to join Arthur's vaunted Round Table. Though Guenevere at first dislikes him, his impressive words and actions soon win her over. They fall in love, but struggle between their feelings for each other and their loyalty to King Arthur. For his part, Arthur knows of their secret love, but hides any knowledge to avoid scandal in the kingdom. However, the lovers' secret is eventually exposed by Arthur's illegitimate son, and Guenevere is sentenced to death. Lancelot arrives at the last moment to save her; he takes her to France, which in turn leads to war between the two countries. Arthur sees many of his best knights killed in battle, and laments at how far things have come. A young boy wishing to join the Round Table approaches and, after being knighted by Arthur, is sent out to tell the world of the dream that was Camelot.

Though it met with mixed reviews and was not initially a hit, *Camelot* received a huge boost when it was featured on Ed Sullivan's popular television show. It was also bolstered by a stellar cast, including Richard Burton (Arthur), Julie Andrews (Guenevere) and newcomer Robert Goulet in a star-making turn as Sir Lancelot. The show was nominated for five Tony Awards and picked up four wins, including Burton's award for Best Actor.

The Fantasticks

The Fantasticks opened on May 3, 1960 at the Greenwich Village Theatre in New York City and ran for 17,162 performances before closing on January 13, 2002.

The musical opens with the Narrator singing "Try to Remember." The song urges the audience to remember the simplicity of youth and young love. At the end of the song, he introduces the four main characters: a boy (Matt), a girl (Luisa), and their fathers (Hucklebee and Bellomy). Banking on the principle that children will do what their parents tell them not to do ("Never Say No"), the fathers build a wall between their houses to ensure that their children fall in love. When Luisa turns 16, her desire for love grows strong ("Much More"). The fathers stage an abduction so that Matt may rescue Luisa and "win" the approval of her father. The plan works beautifully, and Act One ends happily.

In Act Two, Matt and Luisa learn of the set up. Angered that he was tricked, Matt leaves to experience the world ("I Can See It"). Meanwhile, Luisa is seduced by the mysterious but very charming El Gallo, who is played by the Narrator. Both Matt and Luisa are scorned by "the real world," so they return home. Much wiser from their experiences, they reunite and fall in love…again ("They Were You").

In addition to being the world's longest running musical, *The Fantasticks* has earned an Obie Award, a Special Tony Award, and the ASCAP-Richard Rogers award for its writers, Tom Jones and Harvey Schmidt. Additionally, Jones and Schmidt were inducted into the Theatre Hall of Fame at the Gershwin Theatre in 1999.

Gypsy

Gypsy: A Musical Fable opened on May 21, 1959 at the Broadway Theatre, later moving to the Imperial Theatre. The production ran for a total of 702 performances before closing on March 25, 1961.

The story is based on the real life of burlesque artist Gypsy Rose Lee, although playwright Arthur Laurents instead focuses on the domineering presence of her mother, Rose. Even at the outset, Rose is seen pushing her two daughters—June, the star, and quiet Louise—onto Vaudeville stages across the country. They meet Herbie, a former agent, whom Rose convinces through seductive means to represent the girls' act. Though briefly successful, the act's popularity wanes along with that of Vaudevillian theater, leaving the group poor and often unemployed. Fed up with the lifestyle and constant pressure from her mother, June finally quits the show and leaves forever. Rose is given the choice to marry Herbie and settle down to a normal life, but instead decides to make the neglected Louise into the centerpiece of the act, again beginning her relentless push towards superstardom. The act is once again failing, however, when they unwittingly end up at a burlesque house. The manager informs them that his star stripper has been arrested and cannot perform, and Rose volunteers Louise to fill in for the performance. Disgusted, Herbie finally leaves Rose once and for all. Louise, still seeking validation from her mother, reluctantly agrees to do the striptease—and Gypsy is born. She soon becomes a star of burlesque, and no longer needs her mother's help, nor desires her company. Rose, abandoned, takes the spotlight and demands the audience's attention that she feels she was always owed. After her self-righteous nervous breakdown, Louise enters, offering perhaps the hope of reconciliation.

Gypsy was nominated for eight Tony Awards in 1959, but came away with no wins as the awards were dominated by *The Sound of Music*. The show has steadily grown in stature, and was called "one of the most enduring creations of the American theater" by *The New York Times*. The role of Rose has been taken on by such leading ladies as Ethel Merman (the original cast), Rosalind Russell (the film), Angela Lansbury, Tyne Daly, Bette Midler (TV film), Bernadette Peters, and Patti LuPone.

Mamma Mia!

Mamma Mia! debuted on Broadway in 2001 at the Winter Garden Theatre in New York City, where it is still enjoying an overwhelmingly successful run as of this writing. The show has already surpassed the original Broadway runs of many classic hits such as *The Sound of Music*, *The King and I*, *Annie* and *Cabaret*, currently making it the 19th longest running show on Broadway. Additionally, the London production of *Mamma Mia!* celebrated its 3,500th performance in August 2007, becoming the longest running show at the Prince of Wales Theatre in the West End.

Writer Catherine Johnson's lighthearted story is based on the songs of the Swedish pop group ABBA, and features numerous hits including "Dancing Queen," "Take a Chance on Me," "S.O.S.," and many more. The story takes place on a Greek island, where Donna runs a small cafe. Her daughter Sophie, who is engaged to be married, is on a quest to discover the identity of her father. Since Donna won't discuss her past, Sophie reads her mother's old diaries, which describe dates with three men named Harry, Bill and Sam. Convinced that one of these men is her father, Sophie invites all three to her upcoming wedding. After the men arrive, there is much speculation and each man believes he is going to give Sophie away at her wedding. During this time, it becomes apparent that Donna and Sam are still in love with each other. At the wedding, everyone ultimately agrees that it doesn't matter who Sophie's biological father is, and that each man is happy to be a part of her life. In the meantime, Sophie and her fiancé announce that they're not yet ready to be married, so Donna and Sam take advantage of the wedding preparations and are married instead.

My Fair Lady

My Fair Lady debuted on Broadway in 1956 and had an initial run of 2,717 performances—a record at the time. The original production starred Rex Harrison (Henry Higgins) and Julie Andrews (Eliza Doolittle). Based on the play *Pygmalion* by George Bernard Shaw, it tells the story of the "makeover" of Eliza Doolittle, a poor girl with a thick Cockney accent. Henry Higgins, a professor of phonetics, makes a bet with Colonel Pickering, a fellow linguist, that he can improve Eliza's speech, manners and appearance, all to pass her off as a true debutante. Eliza believes that these newfound skills will change her life completely ("Wouldn't It Be Loverly"). After intense and often times frustrating studies, everything comes together and she "fixes" her speech ("The Rain in Spain"). Eliza attends an Embassy Ball and convinces everyone, even a Hungarian phonetics expert, that she is a debutante. The musical ends with the possibility of romance between Henry and Eliza ("I've Grown Accustomed to Her Face").

My Fair Lady is still a beloved part of American musical theater today with 3 revivals, 7 Tony Awards and 8 Academy® Awards to its credit.

Porgy and Bess

The world premier of *Porgy and Bess* took place at the Colonial Theatre in Boston on September 30, 1935. George Gershwin often referred to his masterpiece as an "American folk opera." It blends the genres of symphonic music, opera, Broadway, and jazz. The first cast consisted of classically trained African-American singers—an anomaly at the time.

Porgy and Bess takes place in 1930s Catfish Row, a fictitious suburb of Charleston, South Carolina. The opera opens with "Summertime," sung by Clara, as the men from the town prepare for a game of craps. Clara's husband, Jake, sings his own lullaby ("A Woman Is a Sometime Thing"). During the craps game, Crown, a lowlife, kills another player. He leaves town, telling Bess, his woman, she has to fend for herself. Bess is left alone, and Porgy, who is handicapped, takes care of her. They express their love for each other in "Bess, You Is My Woman Now" and "I Loves You Porgy."

During a tumultuous storm, Porgy kills Crown, who had returned for Bess, in a dramatic fight. Porgy is arrested and taken away, leaving Bess alone again. Sportin' Life, the town drug dealer, persuades Bess to go with him to New York to begin a new life. The story ends with Porgy, released from jail, setting out for New York, determined to find Bess and win her back.

Though *Porgy and Bess* was initially conceived as an opera, there have been numerous Broadway productions. Additionally, many of the arias, including "Summertime" and "It Ain't Necessarily So," have become standards for jazz musicians.

Ragtime

Ragtime is based on the 1975 best-selling novel of the same name by E. L. Doctorow. The production was written by Terrance McNally (book), Lynn Ahrens (lyrics) and Stephen Flaherty (music). In December 1996, *Ragtime* had its world premiere in Toronto, and a second company followed in Los Angeles in May 1997. On January 18, 1998, it made its Broadway premiere at the newly renovated Ford Center for the Performing Arts where it ran for two years—834 performances—before closing on January 16, 2000. *Ragtime* continues touring with regional theater groups throughout the United States and abroad.

The year is 1906, The Gilded Age, when America promises limitless possibilities of wealth and happiness. The story unfolds in New York with the introduction of characters from three diverse ethnic groups: white upper-middle-class Protestants living pleasant but sheltered lives in a neighborhood with no immigrants or people of color; African-Americans seeking equality, opportunity and respect; and Eastern European Jewish immigrants who sailed to America in search of a better life. *Ragtime* is about individuals from those three groups who cross their cultural, ethnic and socioeconomic barriers, and whose lives come together in the most unforeseen ways. Additionally, the cast includes both fictional characters and historical figures such as Booker T. Washington, Harry Houdini and Evelyn Nesbit, whose real-life circumstances are interwoven throughout the story. Emotions run the whole gamut—longing, love, compassion, frustration, disillusionment, and anger that escalates into violence. The story, however, ends very optimistically with the promise of a brighter future and "New Music" for all.

Ragtime received 12 Tony Award nominations, winning Best Featured Actress (Audra McDonald), Best Original Score (Ahrens and Flaherty), Best Book of a Musical (McNally) and Best Orchestrations (William David Brohn).

The Secret Garden

The Secret Garden musical is based on Frances Hodgson Burnett's beloved children's novel, published in 1909. The Broadway musical premiered at the St. James Theater on April 25, 1991. After 709 performances, the run ended on January 3, 1993.

The story begins in 1906 when 10-year-old Mary Lennox becomes orphaned and is sent to England to live with her Uncle Archibald who has been heartsick since his wife Lily's death 10 years earlier. Mary has difficulty settling into his old house, especially since she hears mysterious crying at night. One day, she learns of Lily's hidden garden, which Archibald has kept locked since Lily's death. Mary asks Archibald for "A Bit of Earth" to plant her own garden, but he refuses—she reminds him too much of his beloved Lily ("Lily's Eyes"). Soon after, however, a bird leads Mary to the key to the garden, but not to the garden door. On a stormy night after hearing the crying again, Mary discovers its source— her younger cousin Colin, crippled and confined to bed since Lily died giving birth to him. When discovered in Colin's room, Mary is warned never to see him again. At the peak of the storm, she runs outside and finds the secret garden!

In Act II, Mary daydreams about "The Girl I Mean to Be" with "a place where I can go when I am lost," although she wonders if the garden is truly that place since it is so neglected and overgrown. With some help from friends, the garden is brought back to life and Colin is taken there in a wheelchair as his mother's ghost sings "Come to My Garden." Colin soon heals from the fresh air and exercise. Upon Mary's urging, Archibald returns home from abroad and finds Colin in the garden completely healthy. Colin even outruns Mary in a race! A changed man, Archibald finally accepts Mary as his own.

The Secret Garden received seven Tony Award nominations in 1991, winning for Best Book of a Musical and Best Featured Actress in a Musical (Daisy Eagan). Later productions ran in Australia (1995) and the West End (2001).

Seussical

Seussical is based on the writings of Theodor Seuss Geisel (1904–1991), the American writer and cartoonist famous for his classic children's books, better known by his pen name—Dr. Seuss. The musical debuted in 2000 at the Richard Rodgers Theater in New York City with a plot combining the themes and characters of Seuss' most famous books: *Horton Hears a Who!; How the Grinch Stole Christmas; The Lorax; Green Eggs and Ham; McElligot's Pool; Oh, the Thinks You Can Think!; The Cat in the Hat* and more.

The main plot of the show mirrors *Horton Hears a Who!* The production begins with an almost empty stage, empty except for the well-known red and white hat worn by the Cat in the Hat. The Cat in the Hat appears and leads a young boy into a magical land ("Oh, the Thinks You Can Think!"). They enter the Jungle of Nool and find Horton the Elephant protecting the people of Who-ville who live on a tiny speck of dust ("Horton Hears a Who"). Horton's neighbor, Gertrude McFuzz, thinks Horton's actions are noble. Consequently, she begins to fall in love with him, but he is distracted ("Notice Me, Horton"). Many adventures follow, and different storylines are woven in and out. In the end, Gertrude confesses her love to Horton ("All For You") and they have a baby—an elephant-bird baby, to be exact. Horton worries that he won't be able to care for a child who can fly, but receives this consolation by Gertrude: "I have wings, yes, I can fly…you teach him Earth, and I will teach him sky."

Seussical has made a splash on Broadway. Dr. Seuss' magical world, the dynamic partnership of composer Stephen Flaherty and lyricist Lynn Ahrens, and a variety of celebrity cast members make for a winning combination.

Sweeney Todd

Sweeney Todd: The Demon Barber of Fleet Street is a "musical thriller," featuring music and lyrics by renowned composer Stephen Sondheim. Based on Christopher Bond's 1973 play, *Sweeney Todd* debuted on Broadway at the Uris Theatre in New York City on March 1, 1979. Directed by Hal Prince and choreographed by Larry Fuller, the musical ran for 557 performances before closing on June 29, 1980.

Set in Victorian London, the entertaining yet gruesome story focuses on a vengeful barber, Sweeney Todd, as he plots to kill a crooked judge who destroyed his family and sent him to prison. The barber's plan for revenge expands to include the murders of several other citizens. Meanwhile, Mrs. Lovett—Sweeney's landlady and owner of a pie shop—figures out a way to dispose of the bodies by adding them to the filling of her popular meat pies! After a bloodbath and various horrific twists, Sweeney ends up a victim as well.

The original Broadway cast included Len Cariou (Sweeney Todd) and Angela Lansbury (Mrs. Lovett), who won her fourth Tony award for her performance in *Sweeney Todd*. The 1979 production garnered a total of eight Tony Awards, including Best Musical and Best Original Score. The show subsequently enjoyed two Broadway revivals, in 1989 and 2005 (with Patti LuPone as Mrs. Lovett).

42nd Street

Words by Al Dubin
Music by Harry Warren
Arranged by Ethan Neuburg

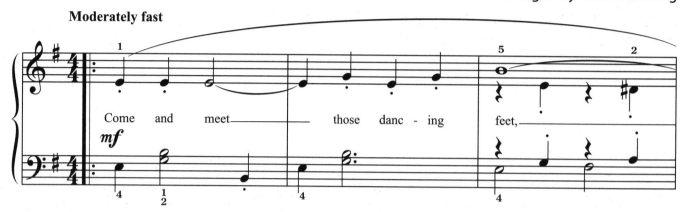

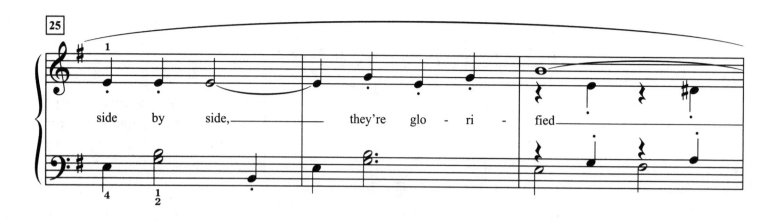

side by side,_____ they're glo - ri - fied_____

where the un - der - world can meet the e - lite,_____

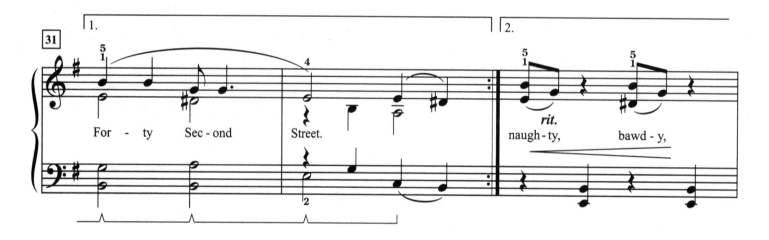

For - ty Sec - ond Street. naugh - ty, bawd - y,

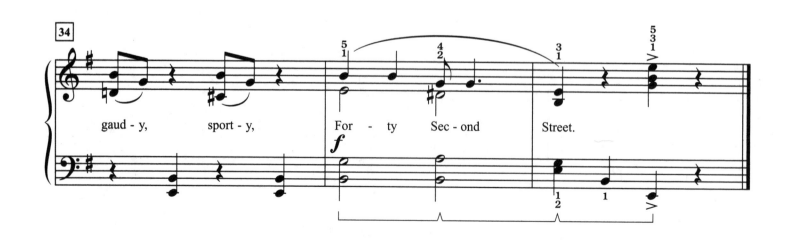

gaud - y, sport - y, For - ty Sec - ond Street.

I Only Have Eyes for You

Words by Al Dubin
Music by Harry Warren
Arranged by Ethan Neuburg

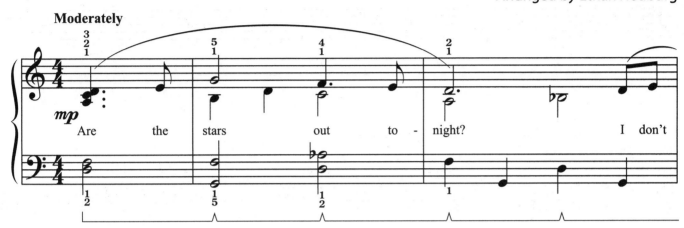

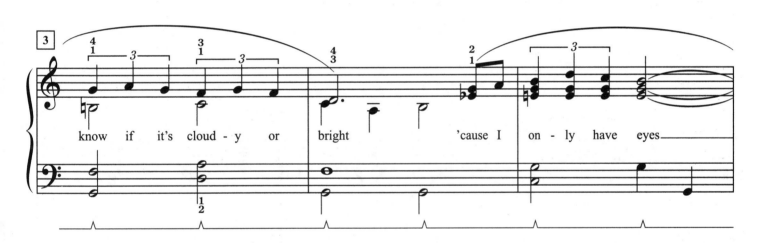

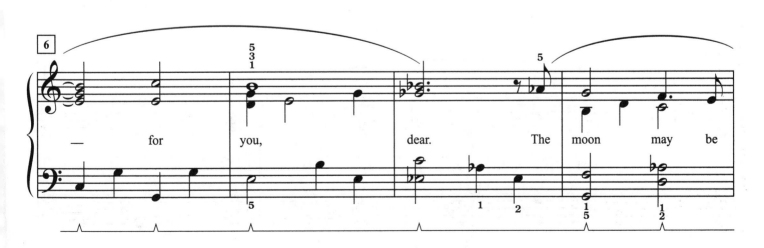

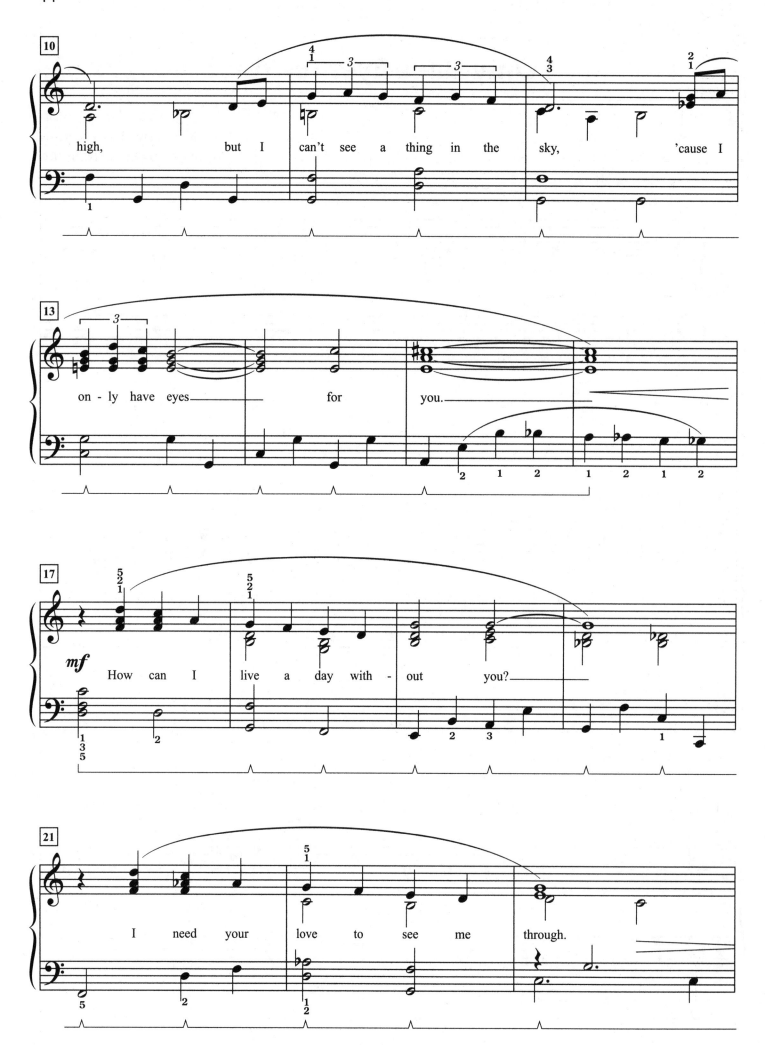

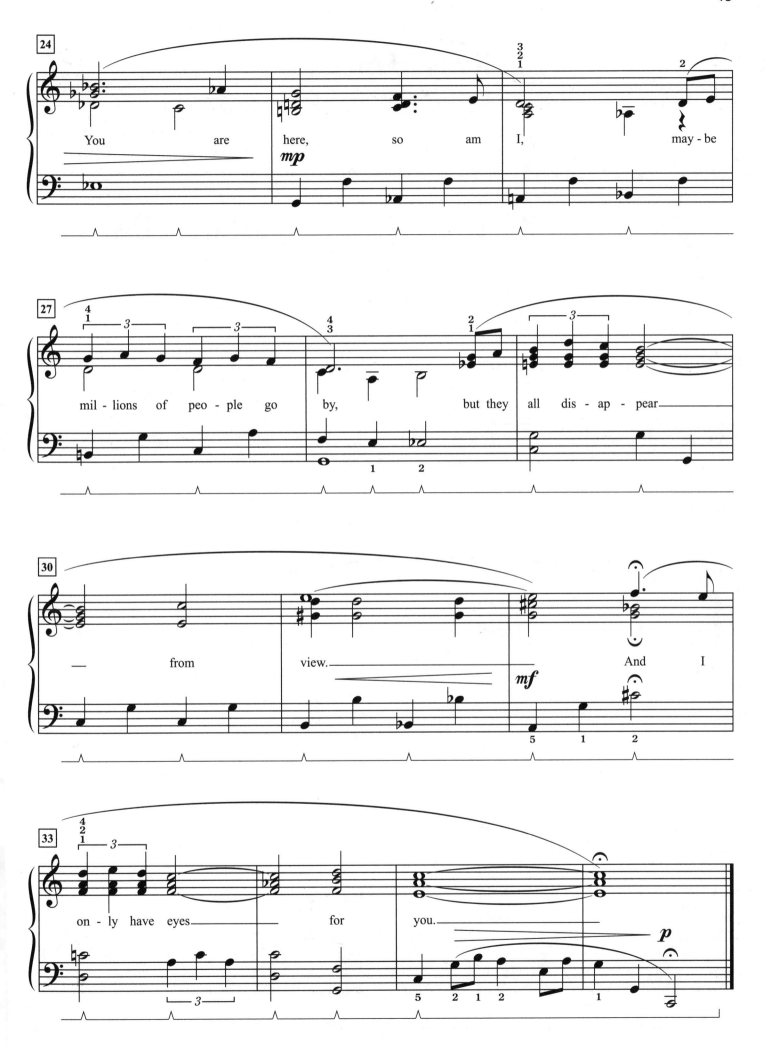

Lullaby of Broadway

Words by Al Dubin
Music by Harry Warren
Arranged by Ethan Neuburg

Moderately fast, with a slight swing

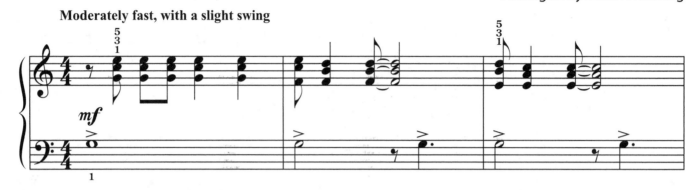

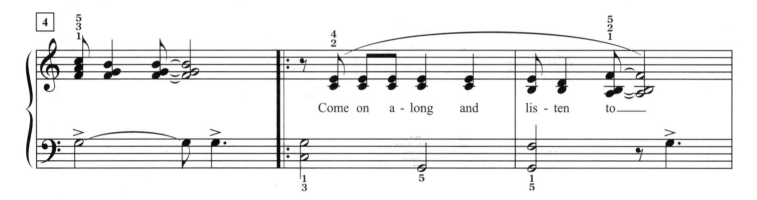

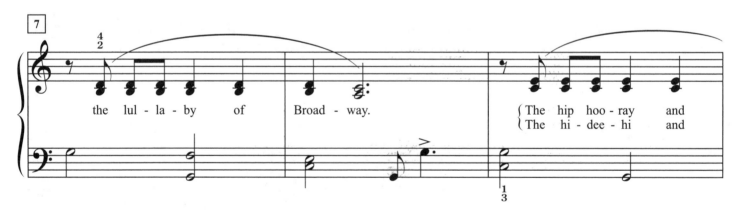

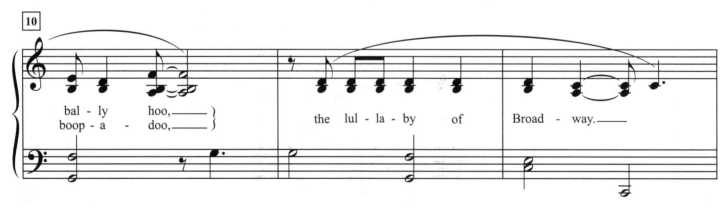

Man - hat - tan ba - bies don't sleep tight____ un - til the
And ba - by goes home to her flat____ to sleep all

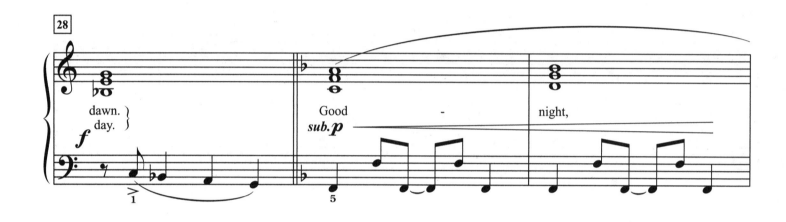

dawn.
day. Good - night,

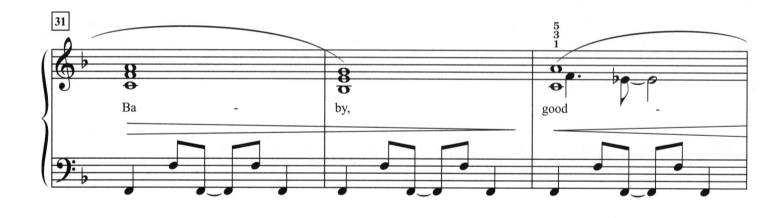

Ba - by, good -

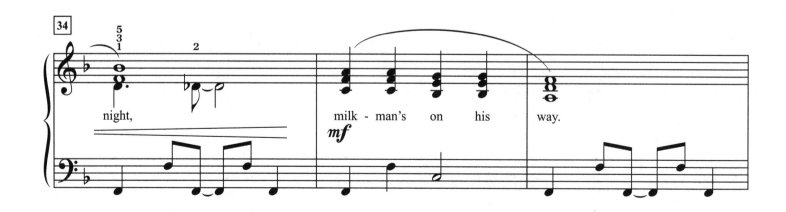

night, milk - man's on his way.

The Gold Diggers' Song
(We're in the Money)

Words by Al Dubin
Music by Harry Warren
Arranged by Ethan Neuburg

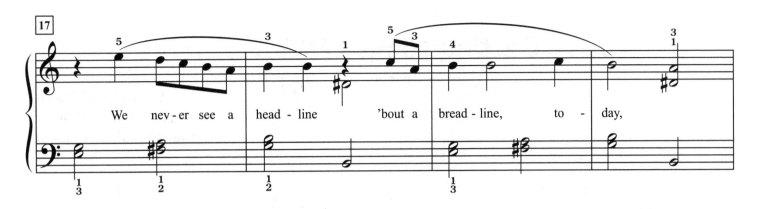

We nev-er see a head-line 'bout a bread-line, to - day,

and when we see the land - lord, we can look that guy right in the eye.

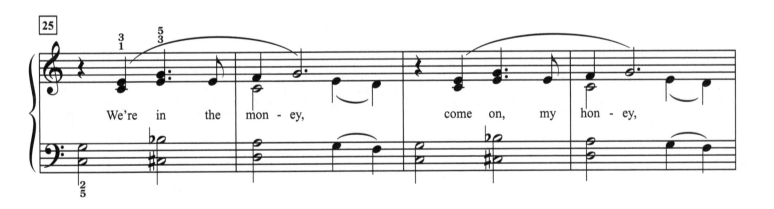

We're in the mon - ey, come on, my hon - ey,

let's spend it, lend it, send it roll - ing a - long!

You're Getting to Be a Habit with Me

Words by Al Dubin
Music by Harry Warren
Arranged by Ethan Neuburg

but now I could-n't do with- out my sup-ply, I need you for my own. Oh, I

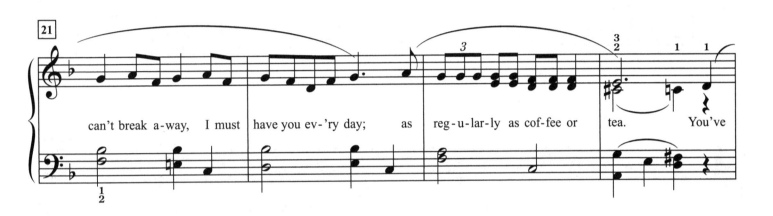

can't break a-way, I must have you ev-'ry day; as reg-u-lar-ly as cof-fee or tea. You've

got me in your clutch-es, and I can't get free;— you're get-ting to be a hab-it with

me, (can't break it!) you're get-ting to be a hab-it with me.

Anything Goes

Words and Music by
Cole Porter
Arranged by Greg Plumblee

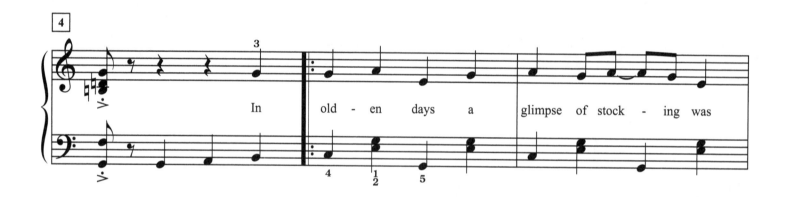

once knew bet - ter words, now on - ly use four let - ter words writ - ing

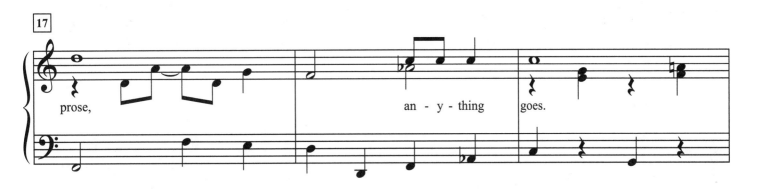

prose, an - y - thing goes.

The world has gone mad to - day,— and good's bad to - day,— and black's

mp

white to - day,— and day's night to - day,— when most guys to - day— that wo - men

cresc.

prize to - day____ are just sil - ly gi - go - los. So

though I'm not a great ro - manc - er I know that you're bound to an -

swer when I pro - pose, an - y - thing

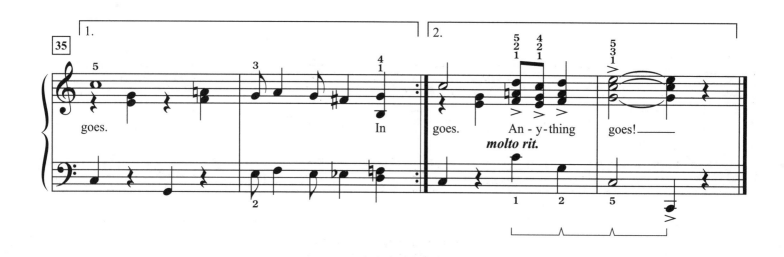

goes. In goes. An - y - thing goes!____

molto rit.

Blow, Gabriel, Blow

Words and Music by
Cole Porter
Arranged by Greg Plumblee

28

Easy to Love

Words and Music by
Cole Porter
Arranged by Greg Plumblee

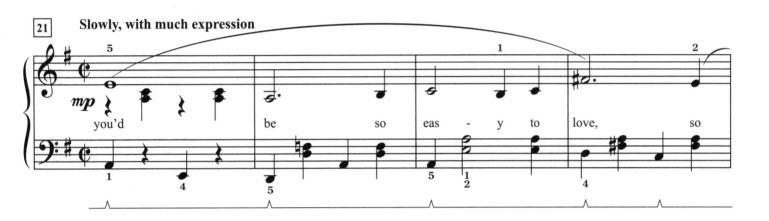

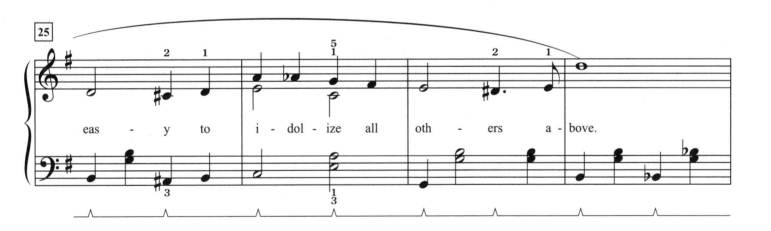

It's De-Lovely

Words and Music by
Cole Porter
Arranged by Greg Plumblee

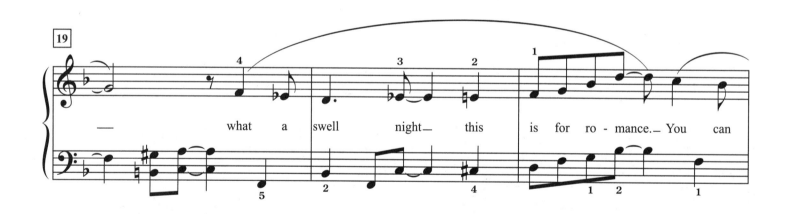

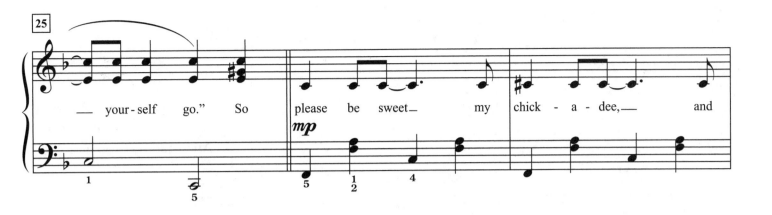

25 — your-self go." So please be sweet— my chick - a - dee,— and

mp

28 when I kiss— you just say to me,— "It's de - light - ful,— it's de -

cresc.

31 li - cious,— it's de - lec - ta - ble,— it's de - lir - i - ous.— It's de -

34 lem - ma, it's— de - li - mit, it's de - luxe, it's de - love - ly."—

f

8va

I Get a Kick Out of You

Words and Music by
Cole Porter
Arranged by Greg Plumblee

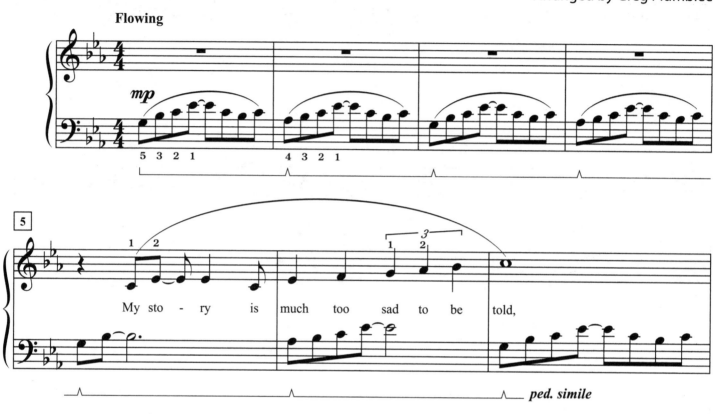

cep - tion I know is the case when I'm out on a

qui - et spree— fight-ing vain - ly the old en - nui,—

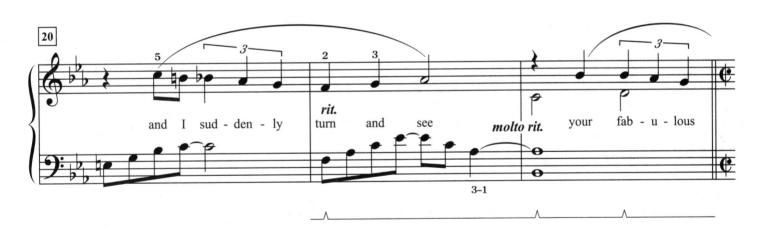

and I sud-den - ly turn and see your fab - u - lous

Moderato (light swing)

face. I get no kick from— cham -

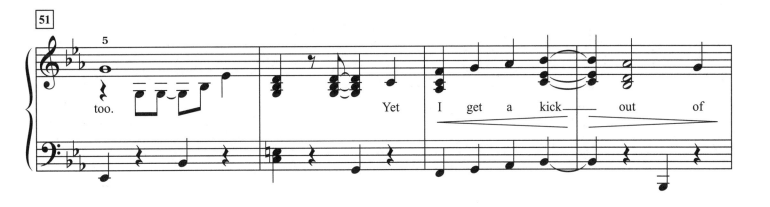

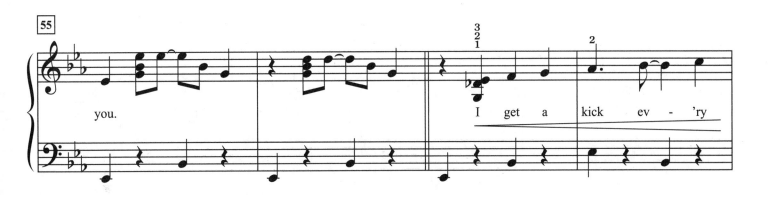

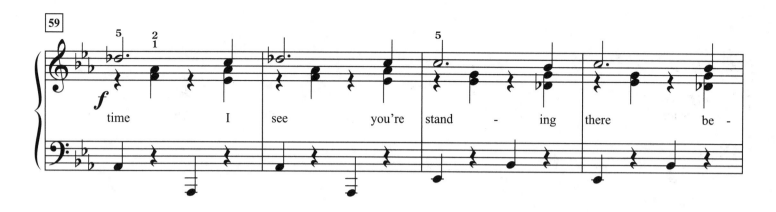

time I see you're stand - ing there be-

fore me. I get a kick tho'— it's

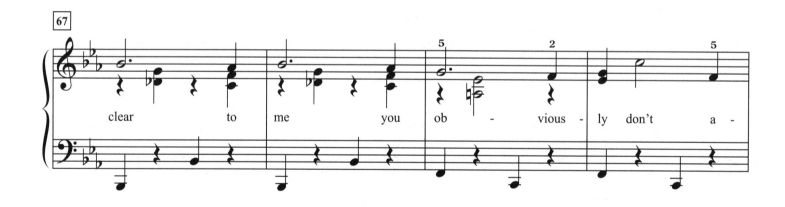

clear to me you ob - vious - ly don't a-

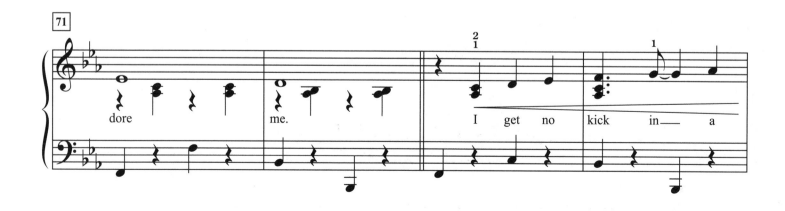

dore me. I get no kick in — a

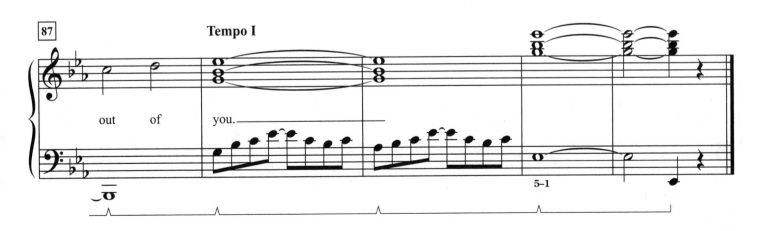

You're the Top

Words and Music by
Cole Porter
Arranged by Greg Plumblee

Quickly

1. At words po - et - ic, I'm so pa - thet - ic that I al - ways have found it
words po - et - ic are not pa - thet - ic. On the oth - er hand, babe, you

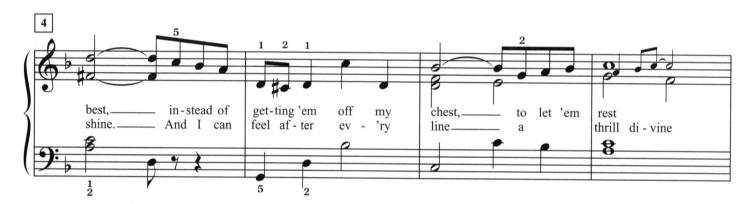

best,＿ in - stead of get - ting 'em off my chest,＿ to let 'em rest un - ex - pressed.＿
shine.＿ And I can feel af - ter ev - 'ry line＿ a thrill di - vine down my spine.＿

un - ex - pressed.＿ I hate pa - rad - ing my ser - e - nad - ing as I'll
down my spine.＿ Now gift - ed hu - mans like Vin - cent You - mans might

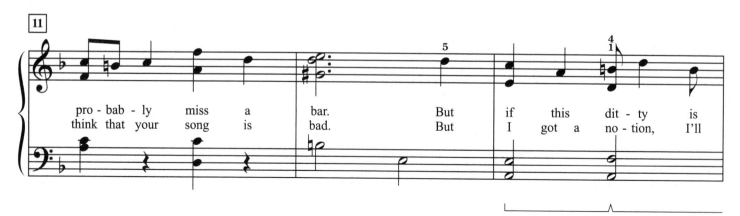

pro - bab - ly miss a bar. But if this dit - ty is
think that your song is bad. But I got a no - tion, I'll

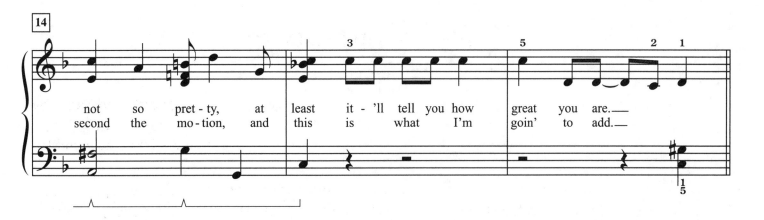

14

not so pret - ty, at least it - 'll tell you how great you are.___
second the mo - tion, and this is what I'm goin' to add.___

17

You're the top! You're the Co - los - se - um.
You're the top! You're Ma - hat - ma Gand - hi.

21

You're the top! You're the Louvr' Mu - se - um.
You're the top! You're Na - po - leon Bran - dy.

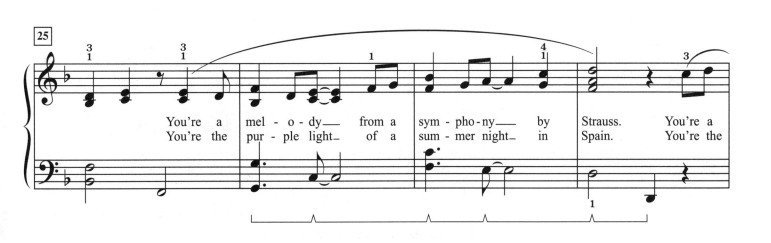

25

You're a mel - o - dy___ from a sym - pho - ny___ by Strauss. You're a
You're the pur - ple light___ of a sum - mer night___ in Spain. You're the

Ben - del bon - net, a Shake - speare son - net, you're Mick - ey Mouse.
Na - tional Gal - lery, you're Gar - bo's sal - 'ry, you're cell - o - phane.

You're the Nile.
You're sub - lime.

You're the
You're a

Tow'r of Pi - sa.
tur - key din - ner.

You're the smile
You're the time

on the
of a

Mo - na Li - sa;
Der - by win - ner.

I'm a worth - less check, — a
I'm a toy bal - loon — that's

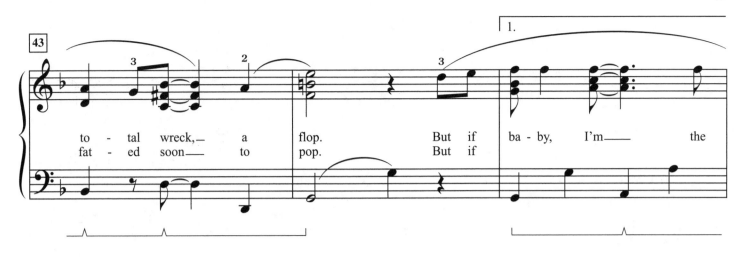

to - tal wreck,— a flop. But if ba - by, I'm— the
fat - ed soon— to pop. But if

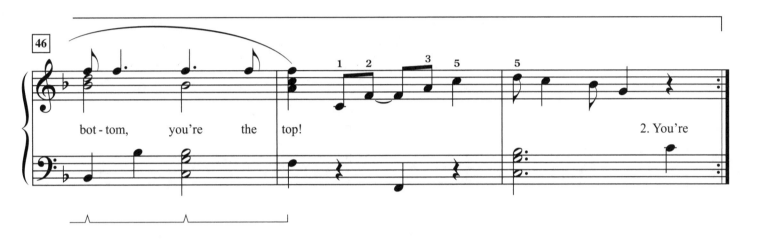

bot - tom, you're the top! 2. You're

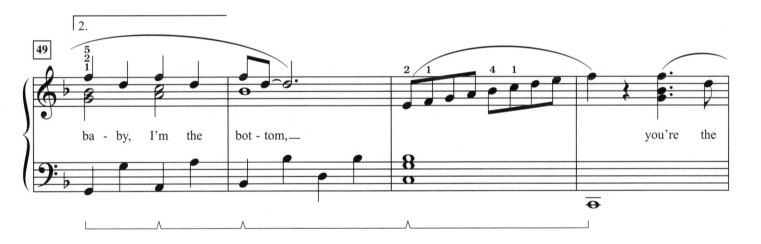

ba - by, I'm the bot - tom,— you're the

top! *cresc.* *ff* *8va*

I Loved You Once in Silence

Words by Alan Jay Lerner
Music by Frederick Loewe
Arranged by Mike Springer

know - ing _____ you loved me too. Yes,

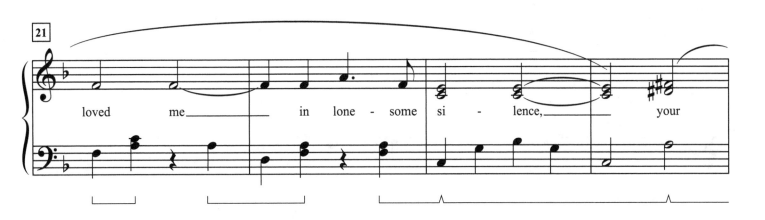

loved me _____ in lone - some si - lence, _____ your

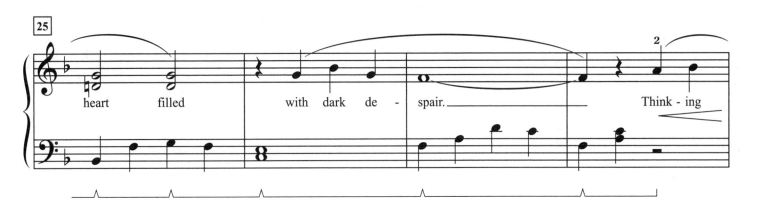

heart filled with dark de - spair. _____ Think - ing

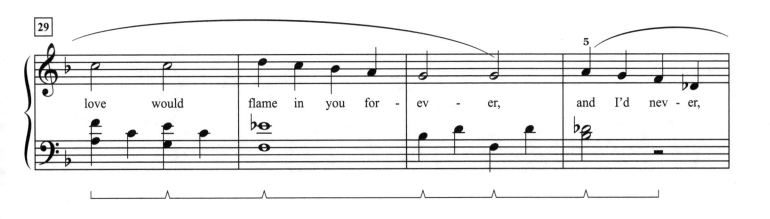

love would flame in you for - ev - er, and I'd nev - er,

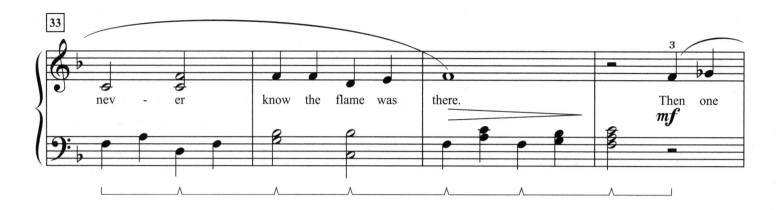

nev - er know the flame was there. Then one

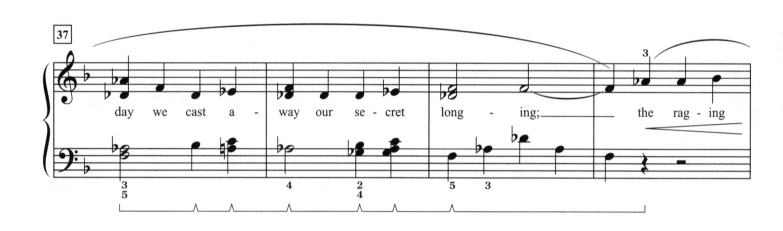

day we cast a - way our se - cret long - ing; the rag - ing

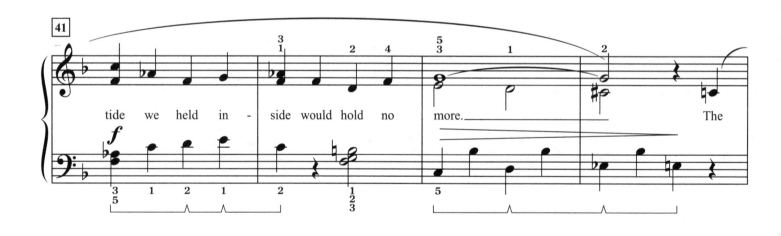

tide we held in - side would hold no more. The

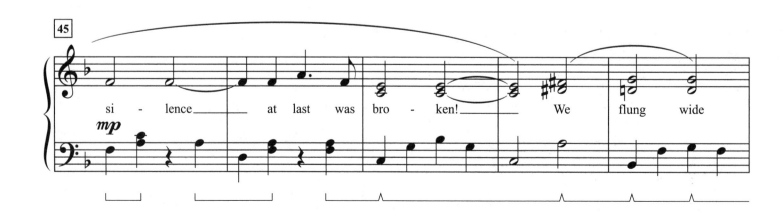

si - lence at last was bro - ken! We flung wide

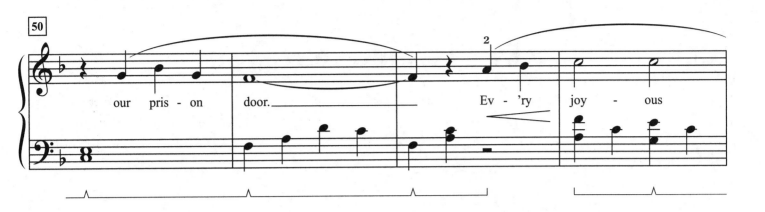

our pris - on door._____ Ev - 'ry joy - ous

Slower, with freedom

word of love was spo - ken. *mf* And now there's twice as much grief, twice the

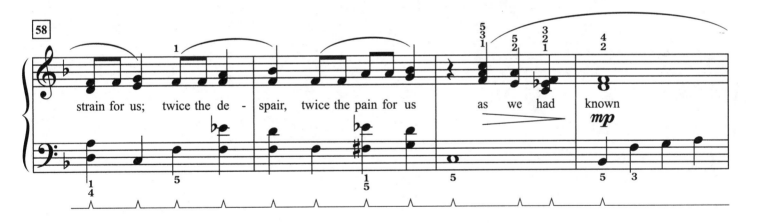

strain for us; twice the de - spair, twice the pain for us as we had known *mp*

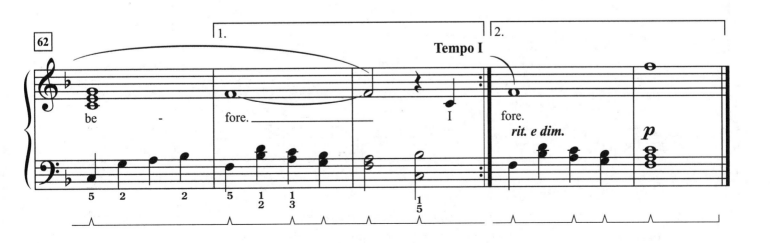

Tempo I

be - fore._____ I fore. *rit. e dim.* *p*

If Ever I Would Leave You

Words by Alan Jay Lerner
Music by Frederick Loewe
Arranged by Mike Springer

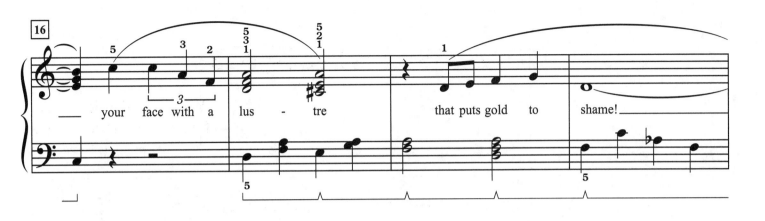

your face with a lus - tre that puts gold to shame!

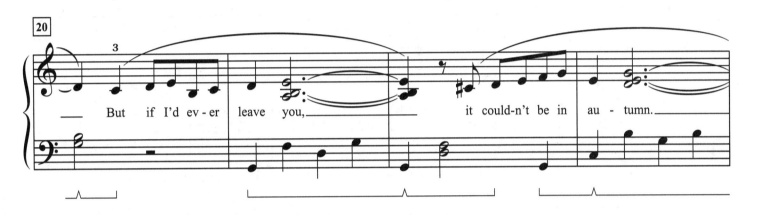

But if I'd ev - er leave you, it could-n't be in au - tumn.

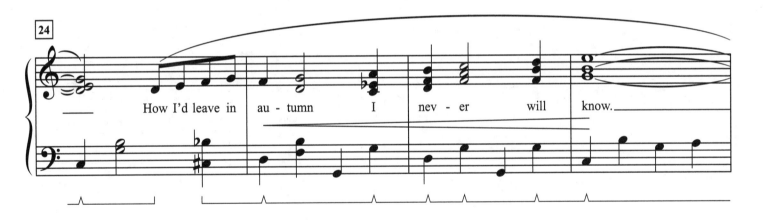

How I'd leave in au - tumn I nev - er will know.

I've seen how you spar - kle when fall nips the air

32

I know you in au - tumn and I must be there.

36

And could I leave you run - ning mer - ri - ly through the snow

_p_

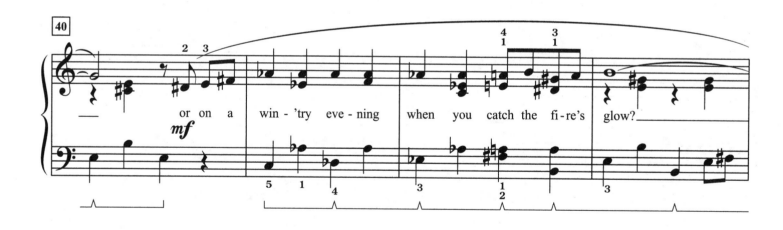

40

or on a win - 'try eve - ning when you catch the fi - re's glow?

_mf_

44

If ev - er I would leave you, how could it be in spring - time,

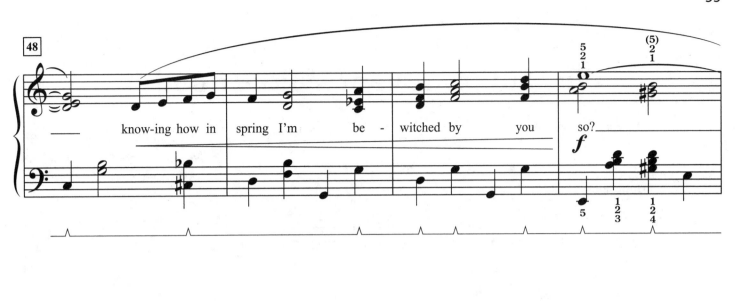

know-ing how in spring I'm be - witched by you so?

Oh, not not in spring - time, sum-mer, win-ter or fall!

No, nev - er could I leave you at all!

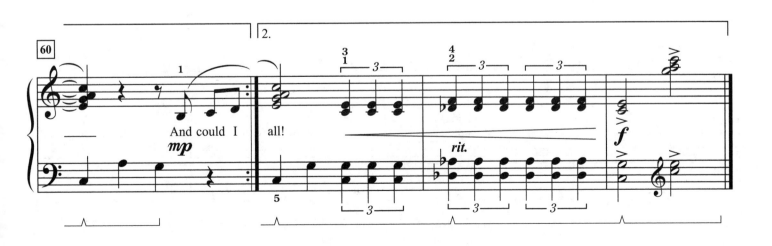

And could I all!

The Simple Joys of Maidenhood

Words by Alan Jay Lerner
Music by Frederick Loewe
Arranged by Mike Springer

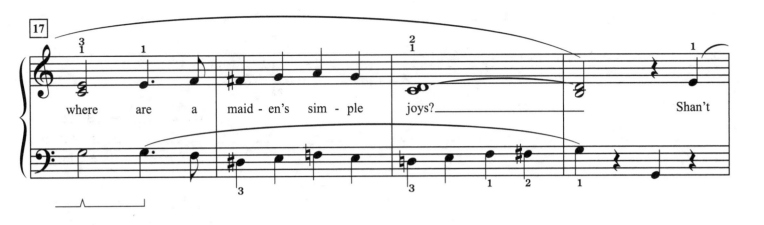

where are a maid-en's sim-ple joys?_____ Shan't

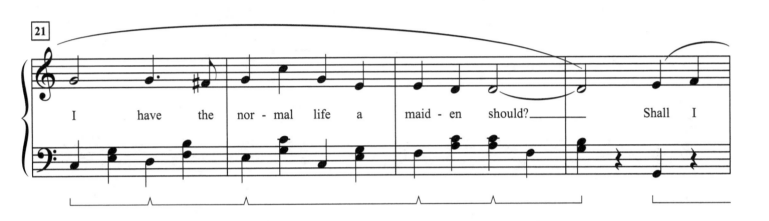

I have the nor-mal life a maid-en should?_____ Shall I

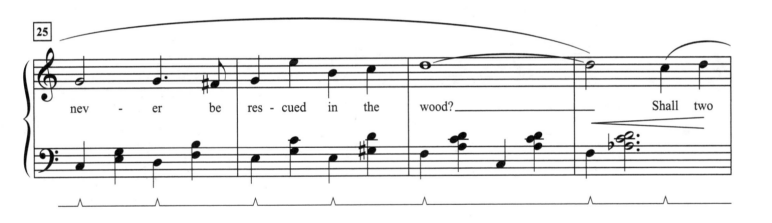

nev - er be res-cued in the wood?_____ Shall two

knights nev - er tilt for me and let their blood be spilt for me? Oh,

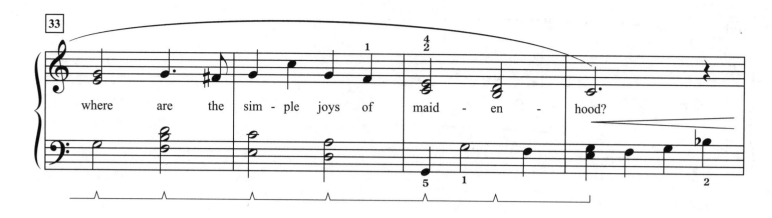

where are the sim-ple joys of maid - en - hood?

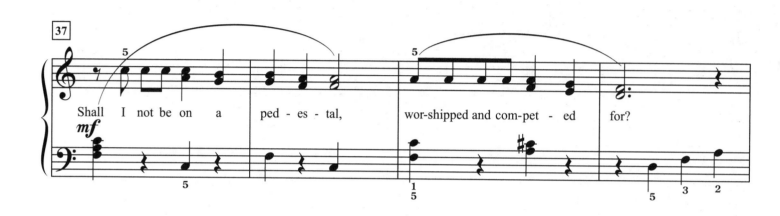

Shall I not be on a ped-es-tal, wor-shipped and com-pet - ed for?

mf

Not be car-ried off, or bet - ter still, cause a lit - tle war?

rit.

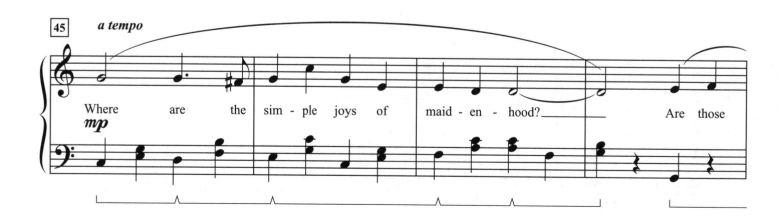

a tempo

Where are the sim-ple joys of maid - en - hood?_____ Are those

mp

Camelot

Words by Alan Jay Lerner
Music by Frederick Loewe
Arranged by Mike Springer

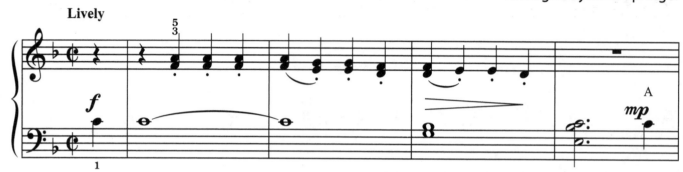

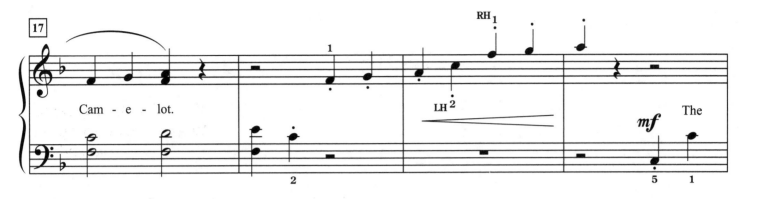

Cam - e - lot. The

win - ter is for - bid - den till De - cem - ber___ and

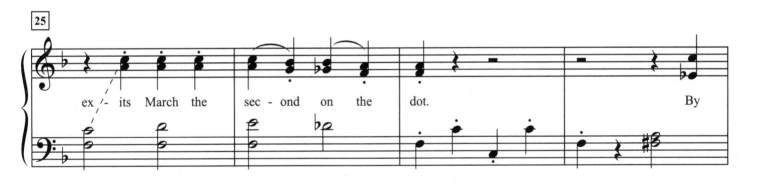

ex - its March the sec - ond on the dot. By

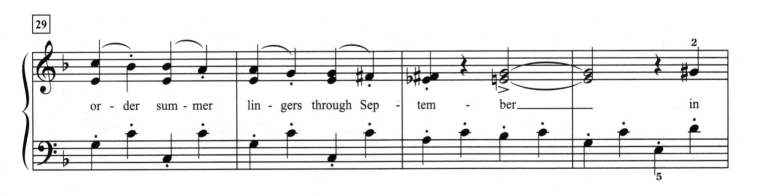

or - der sum - mer lin - gers through Sep - tem - ber___ in

Cam - e - lot.

Cam - e - lot!
Cam - e - lot!

Cam - e - lot!
Cam - e - lot!

I know it
I know it

sounds a bit bi - zarre,
gives a per - son pause,

but in
but in

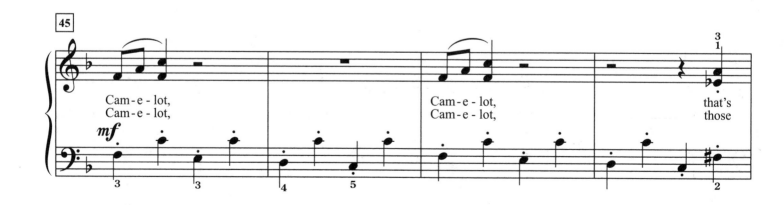

Cam - e - lot,
Cam - e - lot,

Cam - e - lot,
Cam - e - lot,

that's
those

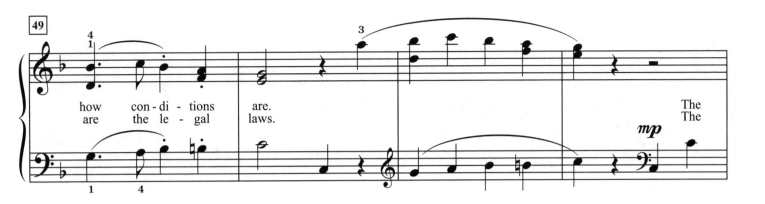

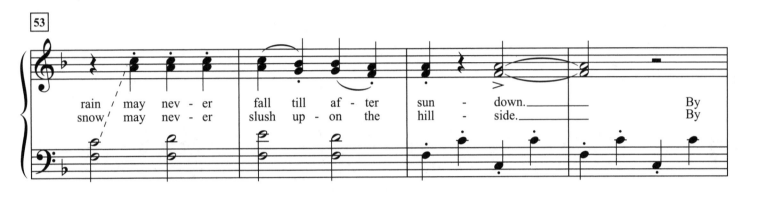

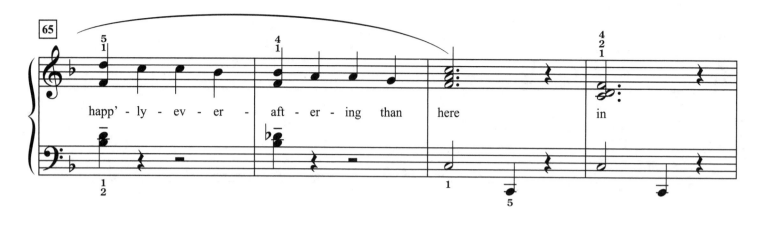

happ' - ly - ev - er - aft - er - ing than here in

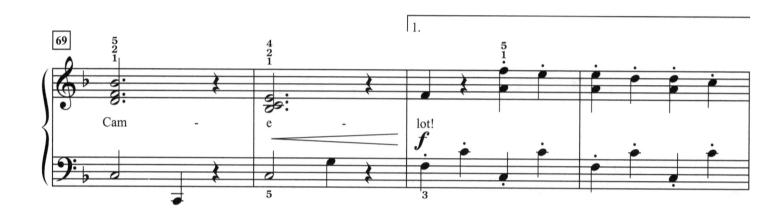

Cam - e - lot!

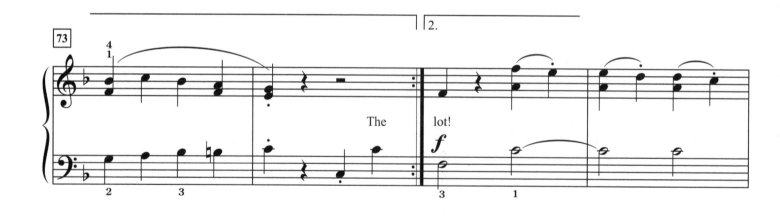

The lot!

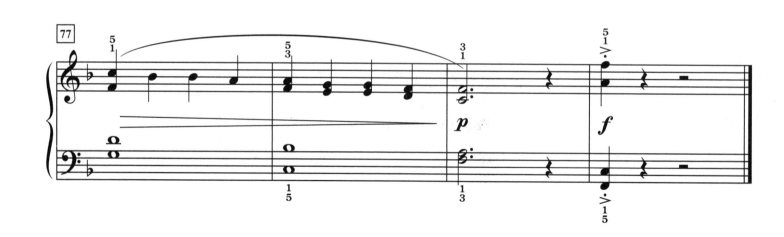

Soon It's Gonna Rain

Lyrics by Tom Jones
Music by Harvey Schmidt
Arranged by Kathryn Lounsbery

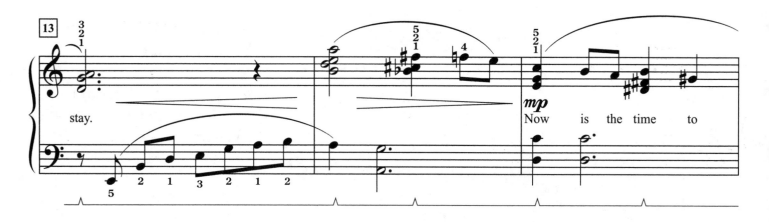

stay.

Now is the time to

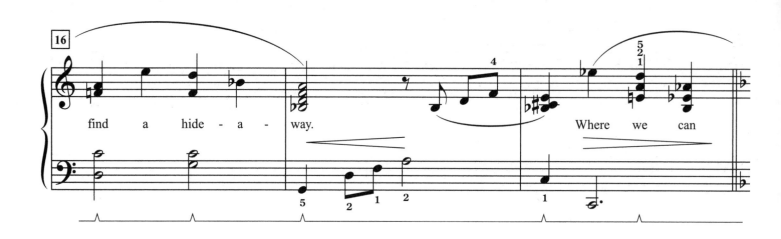

find a hide - a - way.

Where we can

stay.

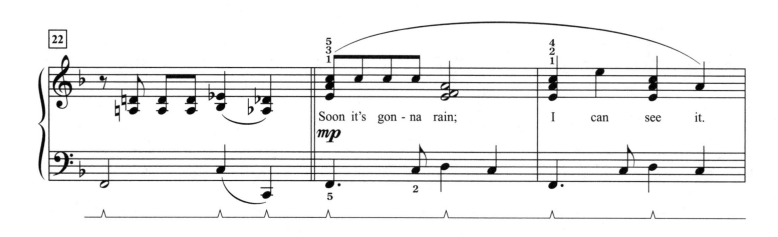

Soon it's gon - na rain; I can see it.

Soon it's gon - na rain; I can tell. Soon it's gon - na rain,

what are we gon - na do?

Soon it's gon - na rain; I can feel it. Soon it's gon - na rain;

I can tell. Soon it's gon - na rain, what - 'll we do with

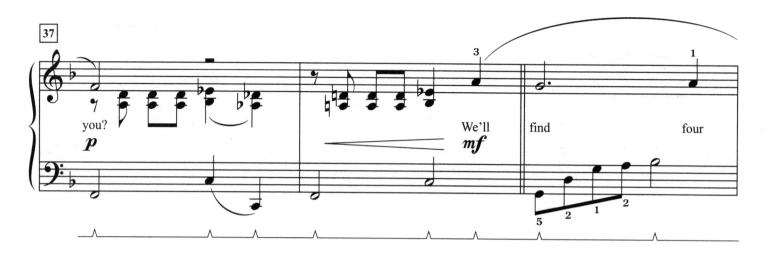

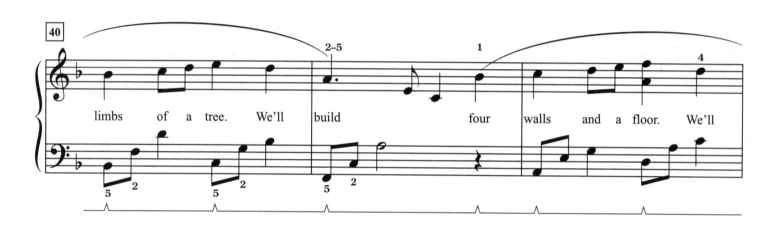

Then we'll let it rain, rain pell mell. And we'll not com-plain.

cresc.

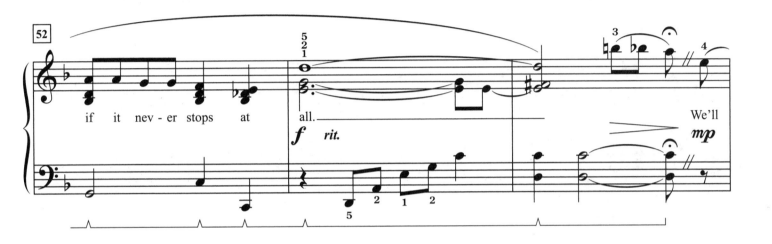

if it nev-er stops at all.

f *rit.*

We'll

mp

Slower

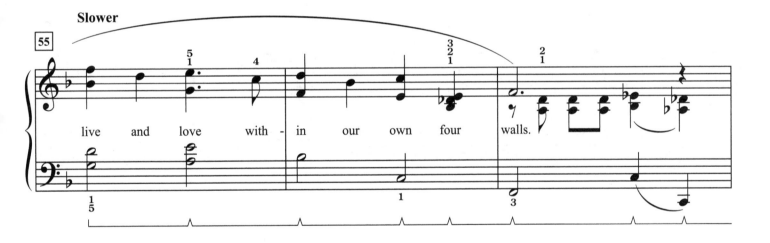

live and love with-in our own four walls.

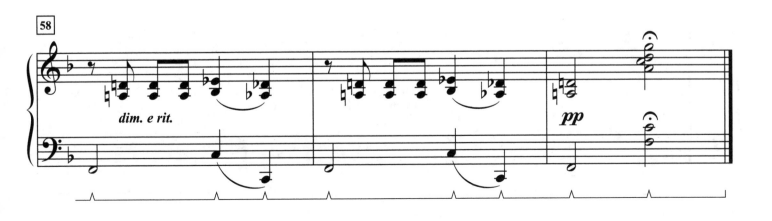

dim. e rit.

pp

Try to Remember

Lyrics by Tom Jones
Music by Harvey Schmidt
Arranged by Kathryn Lounsbery

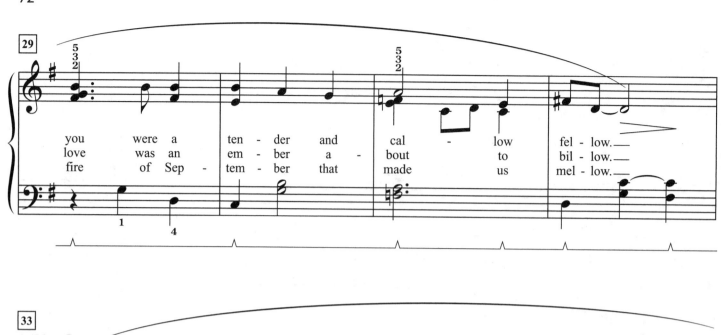

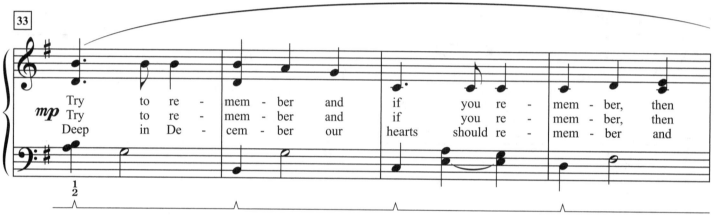

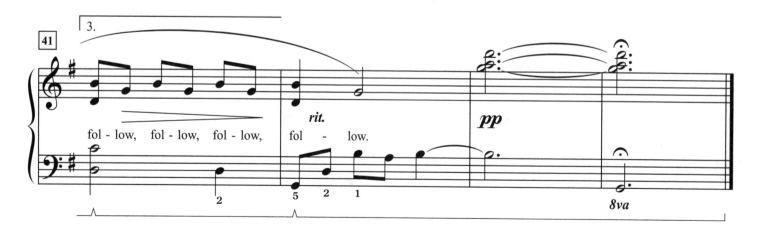

Let Me Entertain You

Lyrics by Stephen Sondheim
Music by Jule Styne
Arranged by Matt Hyzer

Ex - tra! Ex - tra! Hey! look at the head - line. His -

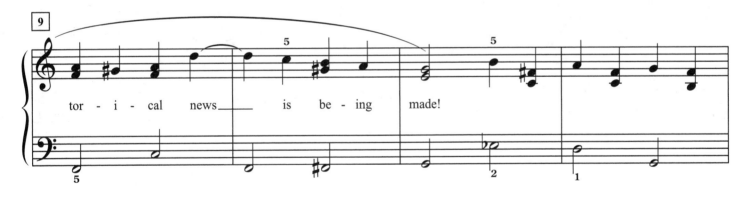

tor - i - cal news___ is be - ing made!

Ex - tra! Ex - tra! They're draw - ing a red___ line A -

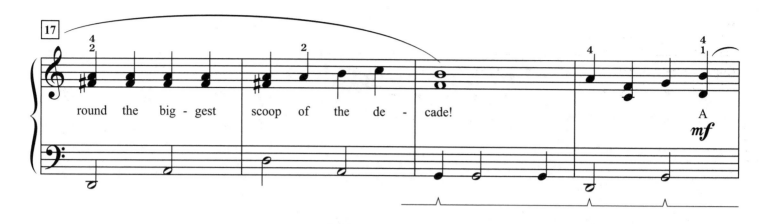

round the big - gest scoop of the de - cade!

A

bar - rel of charm,____ a fab - u - lous thrill!____ The

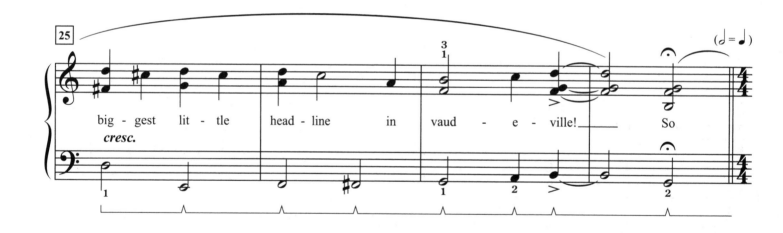

big - gest lit - tle head - line in vaud - e - ville!____ So

Let me en - ter - tain you, Let me make you smile.

All I Need Is the Girl

Lyrics by Stephen Sondheim
Music by Jule Styne
Arranged by Matt Hyzer

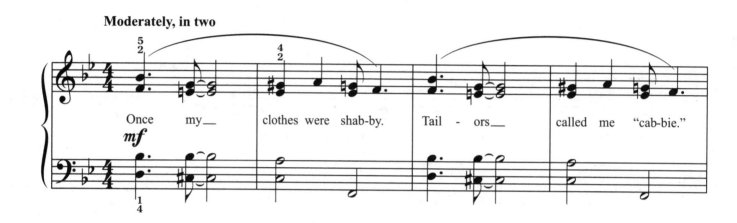

13

I'm the__ cat's me - ow!__ My ward-robe is a wow!__

17

f

Par - is__ silk,____ Har - ris__ tweed.__

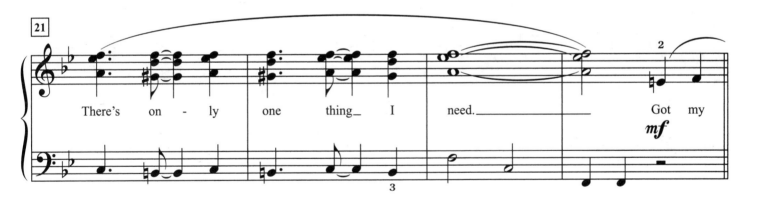

21

There's on - ly one thing_ I need._____ Got my

mf

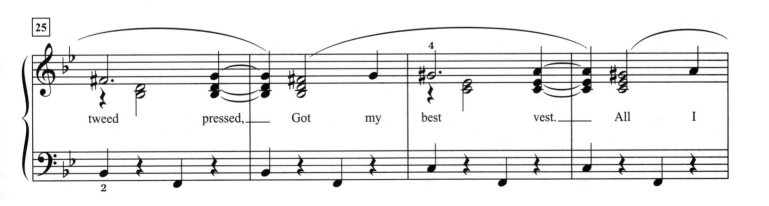

25

tweed pressed,_ Got my best vest.__ All I

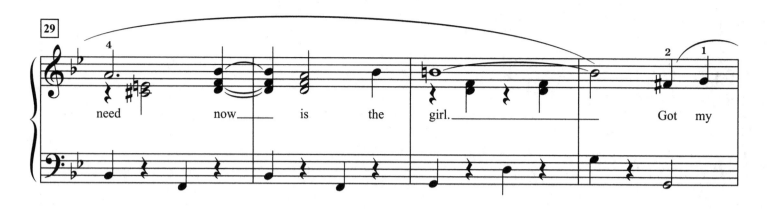

need now___ is the girl.___ Got my

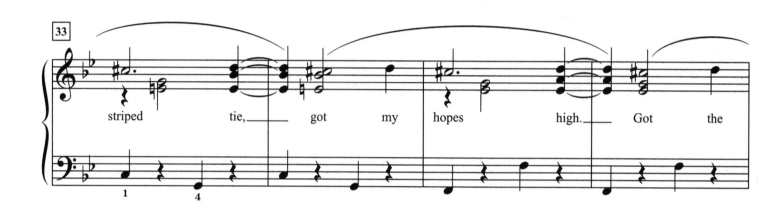

striped tie,___ got my hopes high.___ Got the

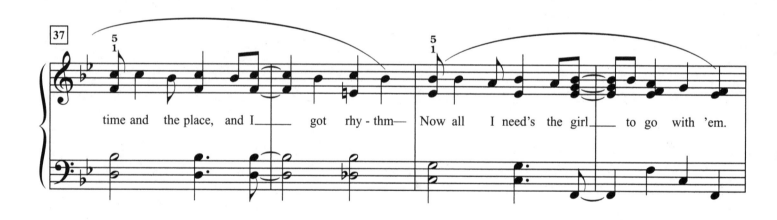

time and the place, and I___ got rhy - thm— Now all I need's the girl___ to go with 'em.

If she'll___ just ap - pear, we'll___ take this

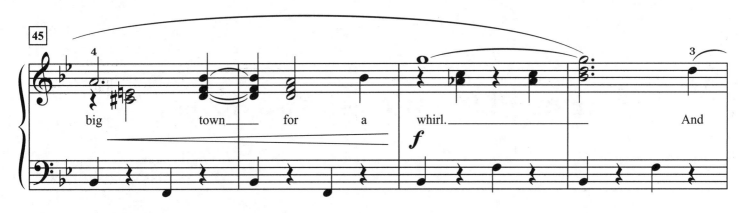

big town___ for a whirl._____ And

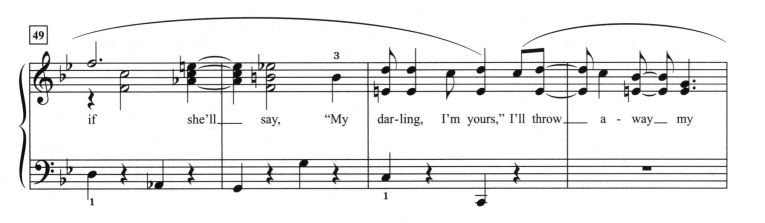

if she'll___ say, "My dar-ling, I'm yours," I'll throw___ a - way___ my

striped tie___ and my best pressed tweed.___ All I

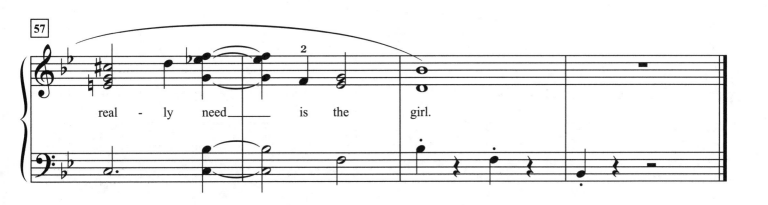

real - ly need___ is the girl.

Everything's Coming Up Roses

Lyrics by Stephen Sondheim
Music by Jule Styne
Arranged by Matt Hyzer

You'll be swell,____ You'll be great,____

____ Gon - na have the whole world____ on a plate!

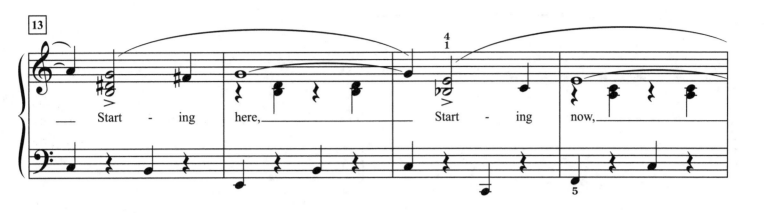

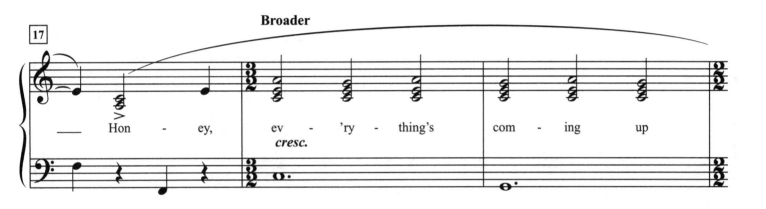

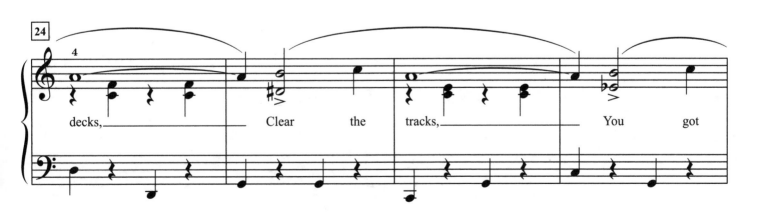

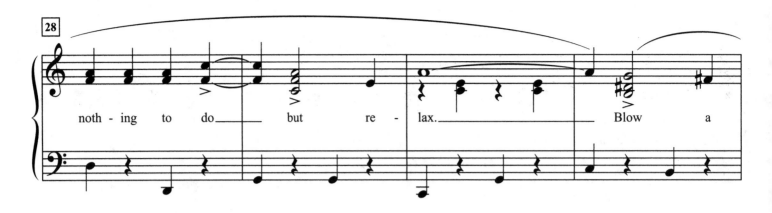

nothing to do___ but re - lax.___ Blow a

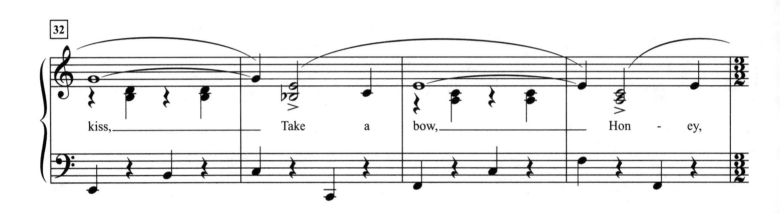

kiss,___ Take a bow,___ Hon - ey,

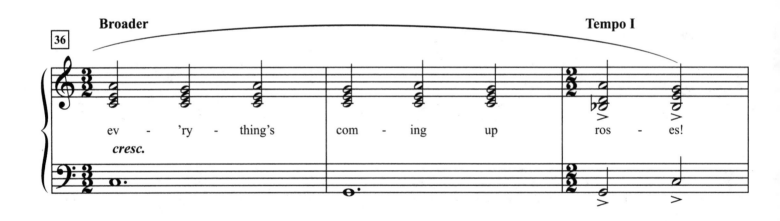

Broader   **Tempo I**

ev - 'ry - thing's com - ing up ros - es!

cresc.

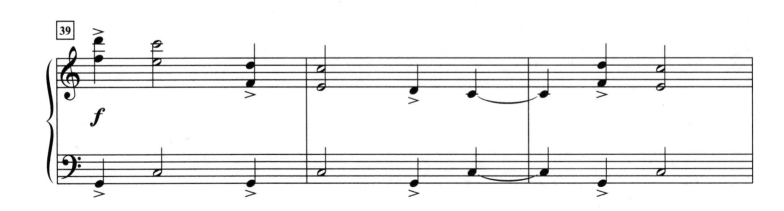

f

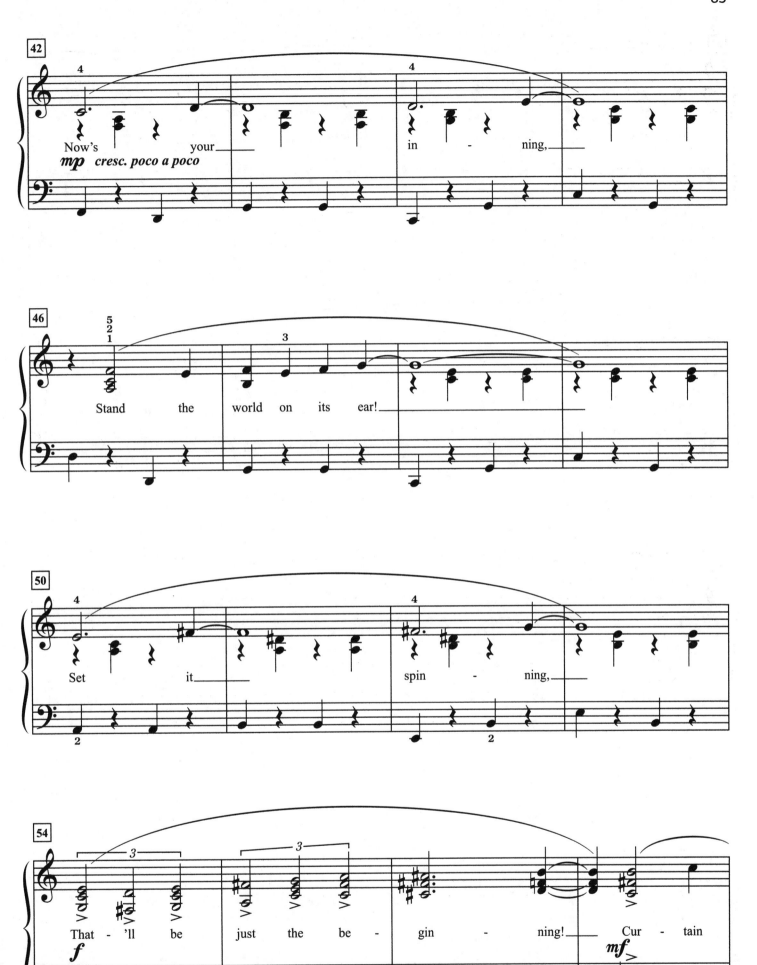

58

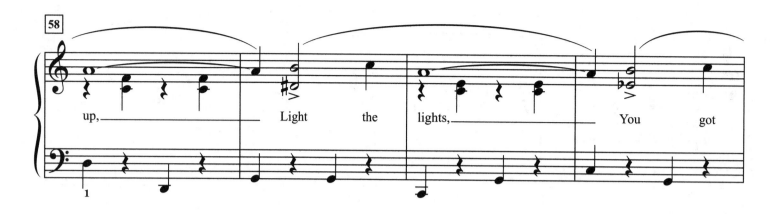

up,_____ Light the lights,_____ You got

62

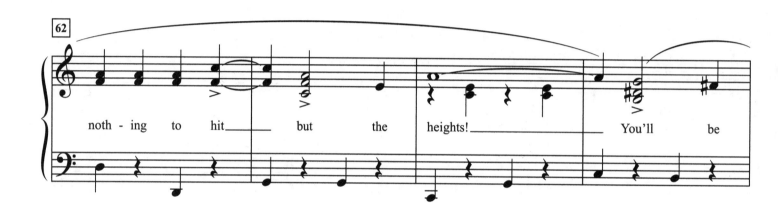

noth - ing to hit____ but the heights!_____ You'll be

66

swell,_____ You'll be great,_____ I can

70

tell,_____ Just you wait!_____ That

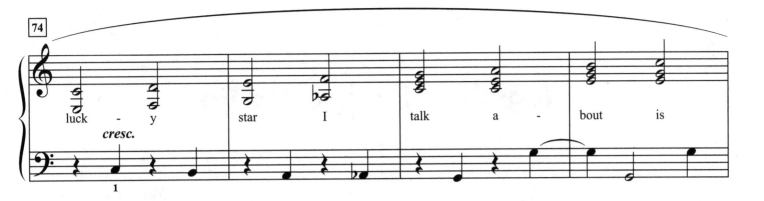

luck - y star I talk a - bout is

due! _____ Hon - ey,

Broader

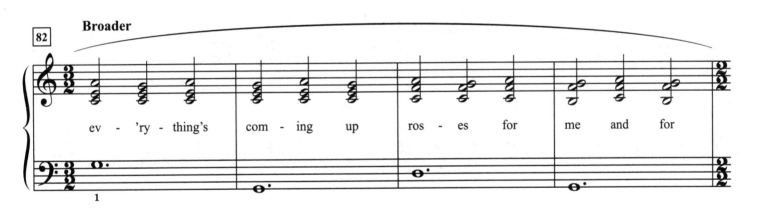

ev - 'ry - thing's com - ing up ros - es for me and for

Tempo I

you!

Together Wherever We Go

Lyrics by Stephen Sondheim
Music by Jule Styne
Arranged by Matt Hyzer

Moderately, in two

may not go far,— But sure as a star,— wher -

ev - er we are,— it's to - geth - er!— Wher -

ev - er I go,— I know he goes.— Wher -

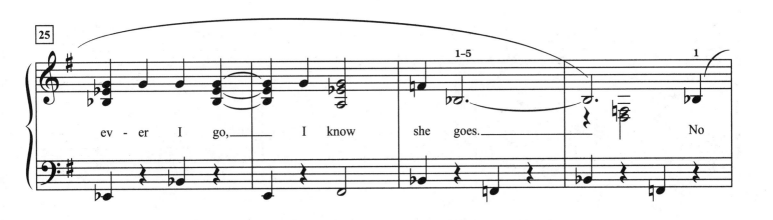

ev - er I go,— I know she goes.— No

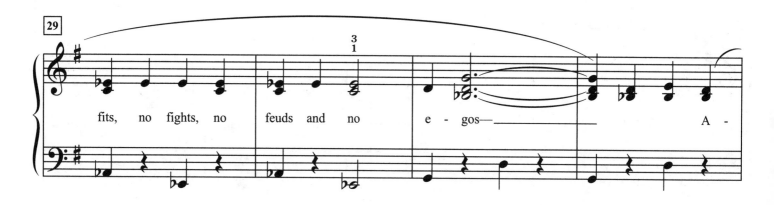

fits, no fights, no feuds and no e - gos_____ A -

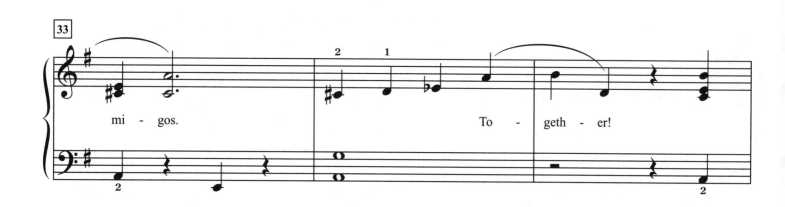

mi - gos. To - geth - er!

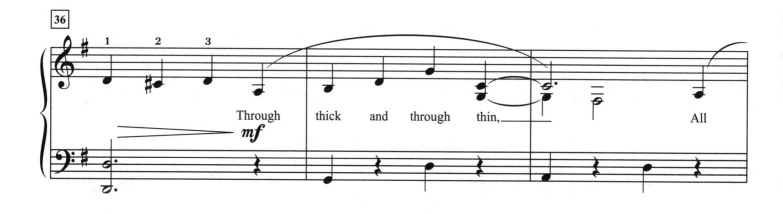

Through thick and through thin,_____ All

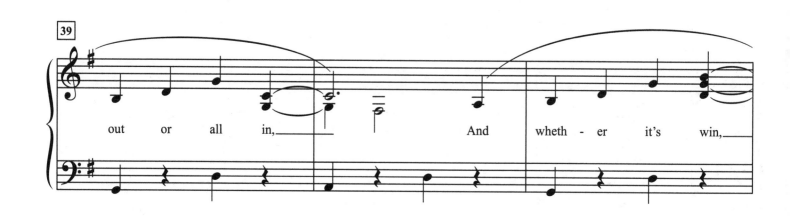

out or all in,_____ And wheth - er it's win,_____

place or show,_____ With

you for me and me for you, We'll mud - dle through__ what - ev -

cresc.

er we do__ To - geth - er, wher - ev - er we

f

go!_____

I Do, I Do, I Do, I Do, I Do

Words and Music by
Benny Andersson, Stig Anderson and Björn Ulvaeus
Arranged by Bill Galliford

it, you love me, don't de-ny — it. Say I do? I

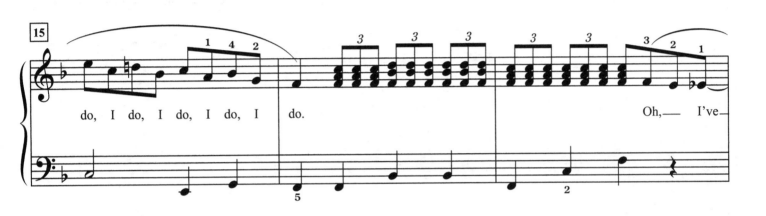

do, I do, I do, I do, I do. Oh, — I've

been — dream - ing through my lone - ly — past.
hard — feel - ings be - tween you and — me.

Now I just made it, I found you at last.
If we can't make it, well, just wait and see. So come

on now, let's try — it, I love you, can't de-ny — it. 'cause it's

true, I do, I do, I do, I do, I do.

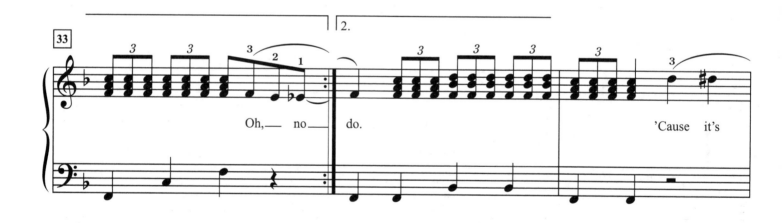

Oh, — no — do. 'Cause it's

true, I do, I do, I do, I do, I do.

Knowing Me, Knowing You

Words and Music by
Benny Andersson, Stig Anderson and Björn Ulvaeus
Arranged by Bill Galliford

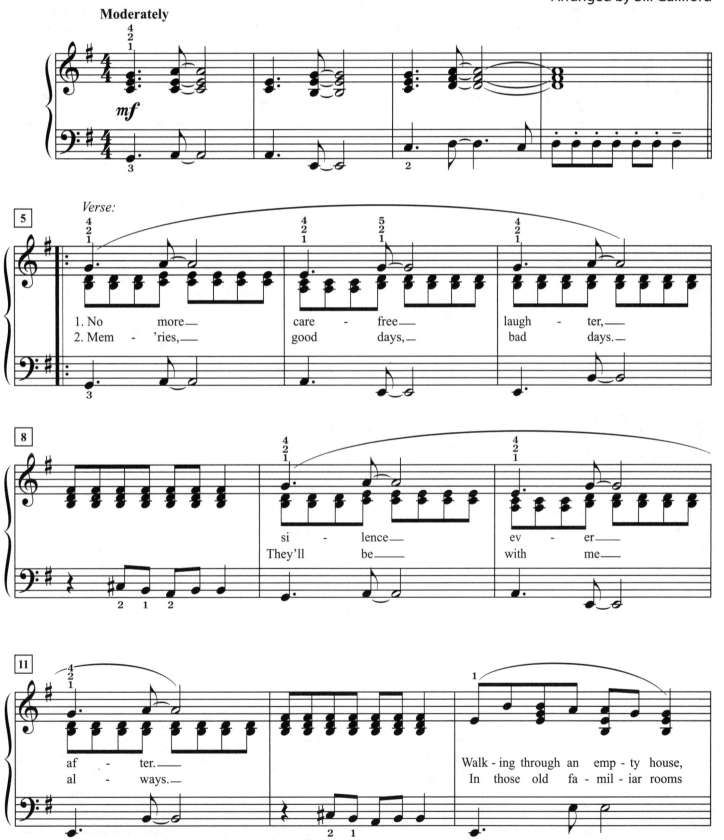

Mamma Mia!

Words and Music by
Benny Andersson, Stig Anderson and Björn Ulvaeus
Arranged by Bill Galliford

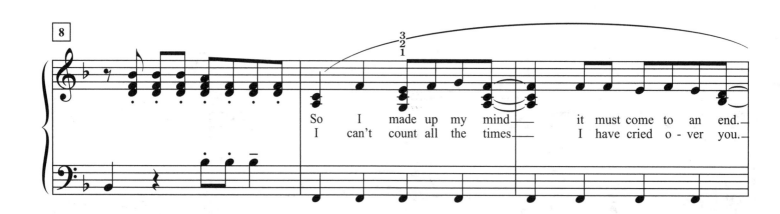

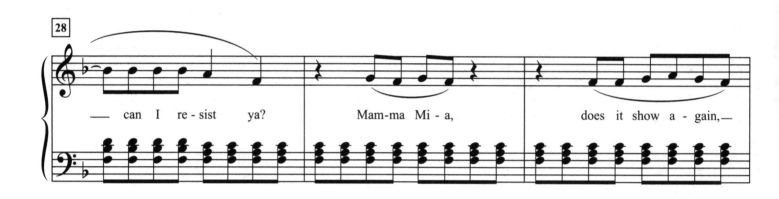

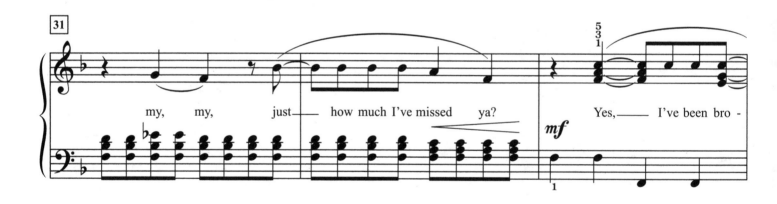

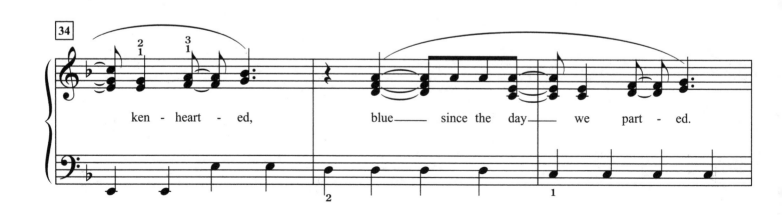

Why, why, did — I ev - er let you go? — Mam - ma Mi - a,

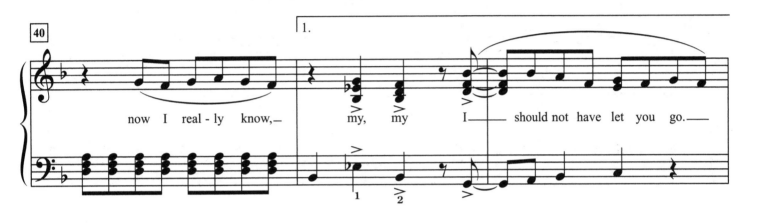

now I real - ly know, — my, my I — should not have let you go. —

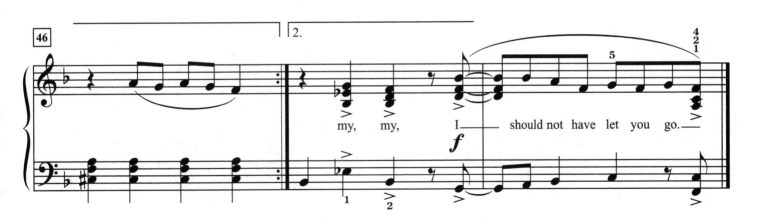

my, my, I — should not have let you go. —

Take a Chance on Me

Words and Music by
Benny Andersson and Björn Ulvaeus
Arranged by Bill Galliford

Slowly and freely

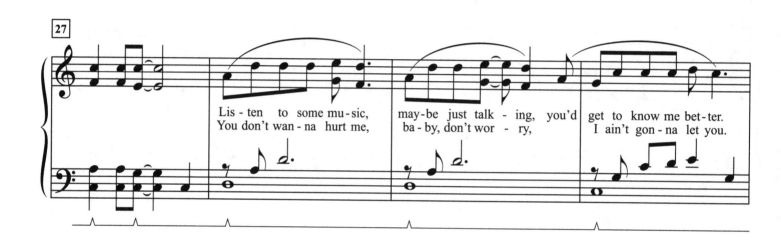

think you know———— that I want you so.——
think you know———— that I want you so.——

to Coda ⊕

Chorus:

If you change your mind,—— I'm the first in line.—— Hon-ey, I'm still free,

mf

—— take a chance on me.—— If you need me, let—— me know, gon-na be a - round.

—— If you've got no place—— to go when you're feel-ing down.——

If you're still a - lone ____ when the pret-ty birds ____ have flown, hon-ey, I'm still free, ____

____ take a chance on me. ____ Gon-na do my ver - y best and it ain't no lie, ____

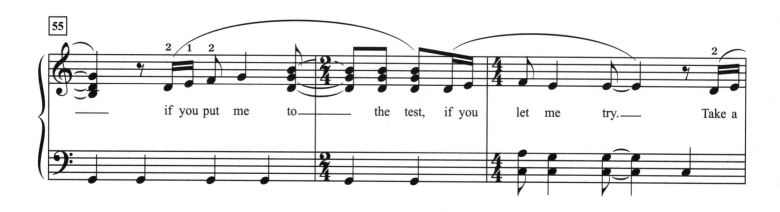

____ if you put me to ____ the test, if you let me try. ____ Take a

D.S. al Coda

chance on me, ____ take a chance on me. ____ 2. Oh, you can

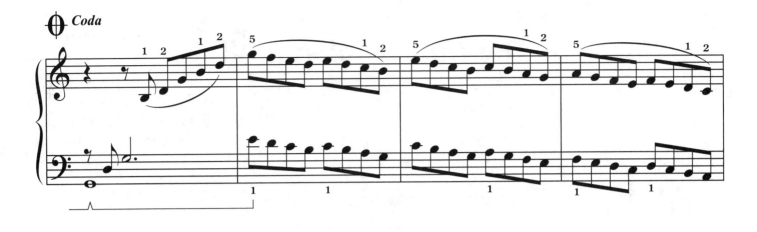

The Winner Takes It All

Words and Music by
Benny Andersson and Björn Ulvaeus
Arranged by Bill Galliford

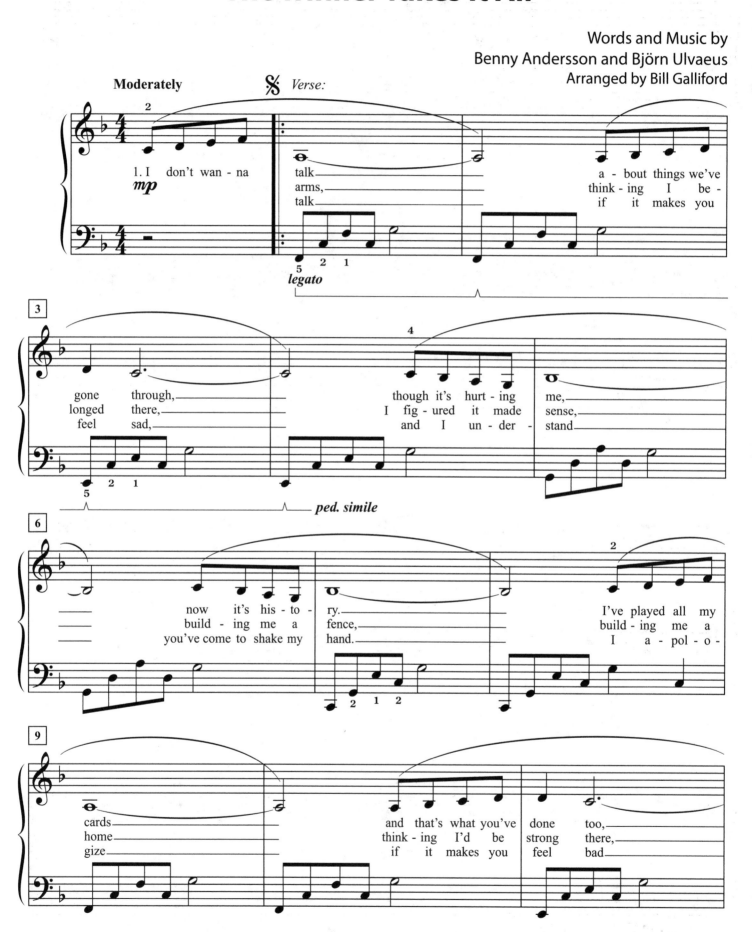

The win-ner takes it all,_____ the los-er has to

fall._____ It's sim-ple and it's plain,_____

why should I com - plain?_____ 3. I don't wan-na

D.S. al Coda

_____ The win-ner takes it all.

The win-ner takes it all._____

The game is on a - gain,_____ a lov-er or a friend,_____

a big thing or a small,_____ the win-ner takes it all._____

The win-ner takes it all. *rit.* *mp*

Get Me to the Church on Time

Lyrics by Alan Jay Lerner
Music by Frederick Loewe
Arranged by Dan Coates

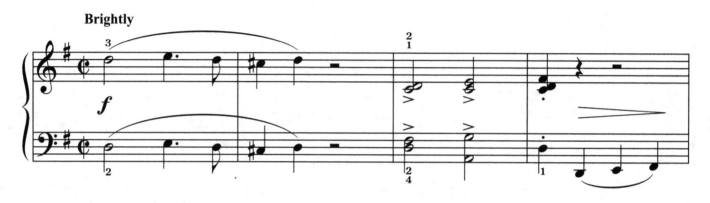

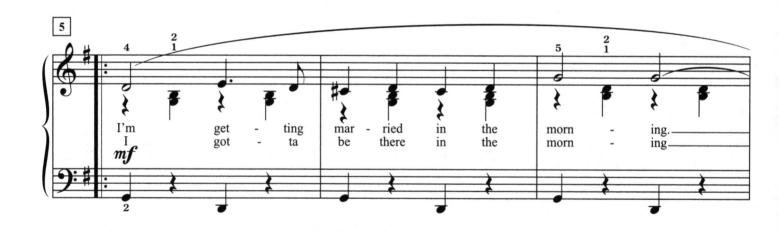

I'm get - ting mar - ried in the morn - ing.
I got - ta be there in the morn - ing.

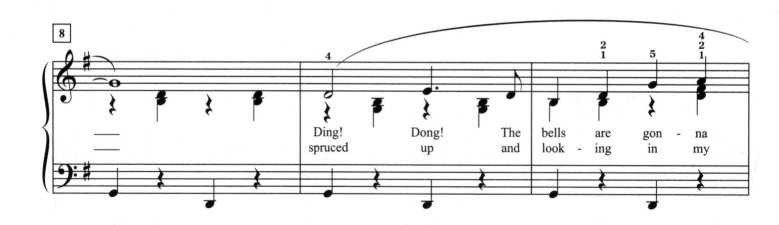

Ding! Dong! The bells are gon - na
spruced up and look - ing in my

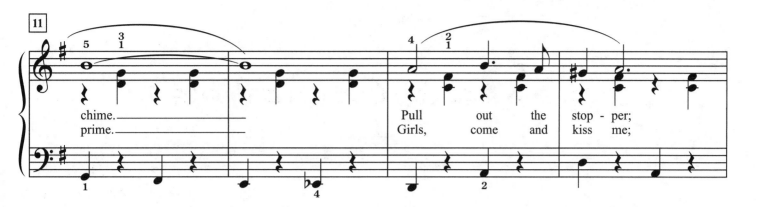

chime.
prime.
Pull out the stop - per;
Girls, come and kiss me;

let's have a whop - per, but get me to the church on
show how you'll miss me, but get me to the church on

time!
time! If I am

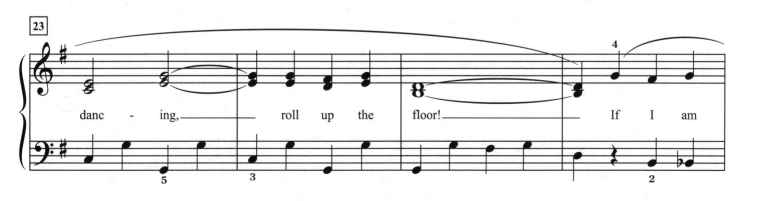

danc - ing, roll up the floor! If I am

whist - ling, whewt me out the door! For

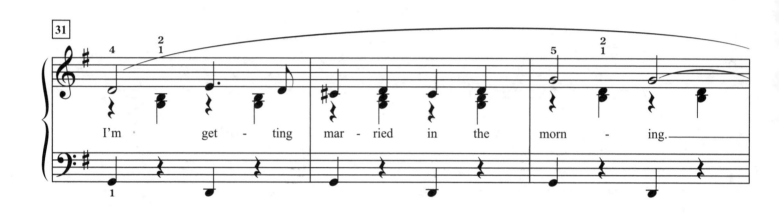

I'm get - ting mar - ried in the morn - ing.

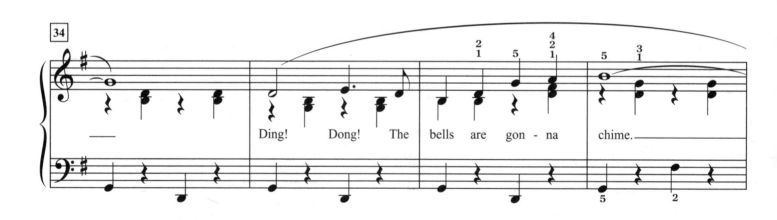

Ding! Dong! The bells are gon - na chime.

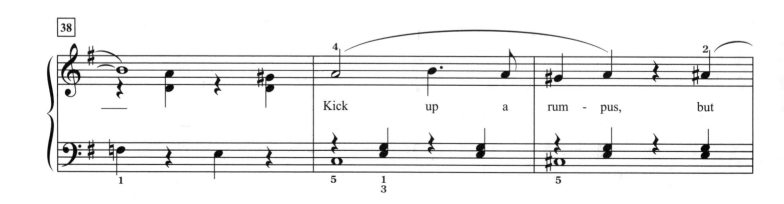

Kick up a rum - pus, but

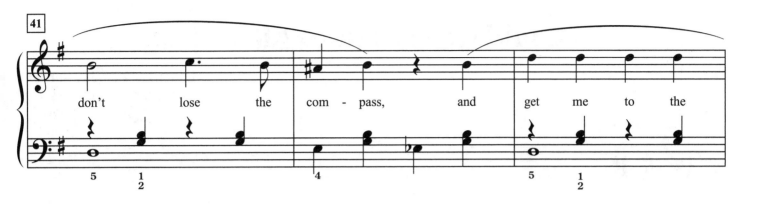

don't   lose   the   com - pass,   and   get   me   to   the

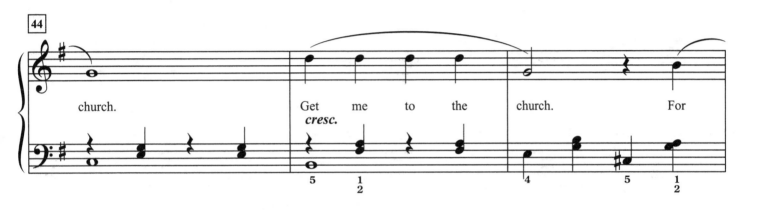

church.   Get   me   to   the   church.   For

cresc.

Pete's   sake,   get   me   to   the   church   on

f

time!

sf

I Could Have Danced All Night

Lyrics by Alan Jay Lerner
Music by Frederick Loewe
Arranged by Dan Coates

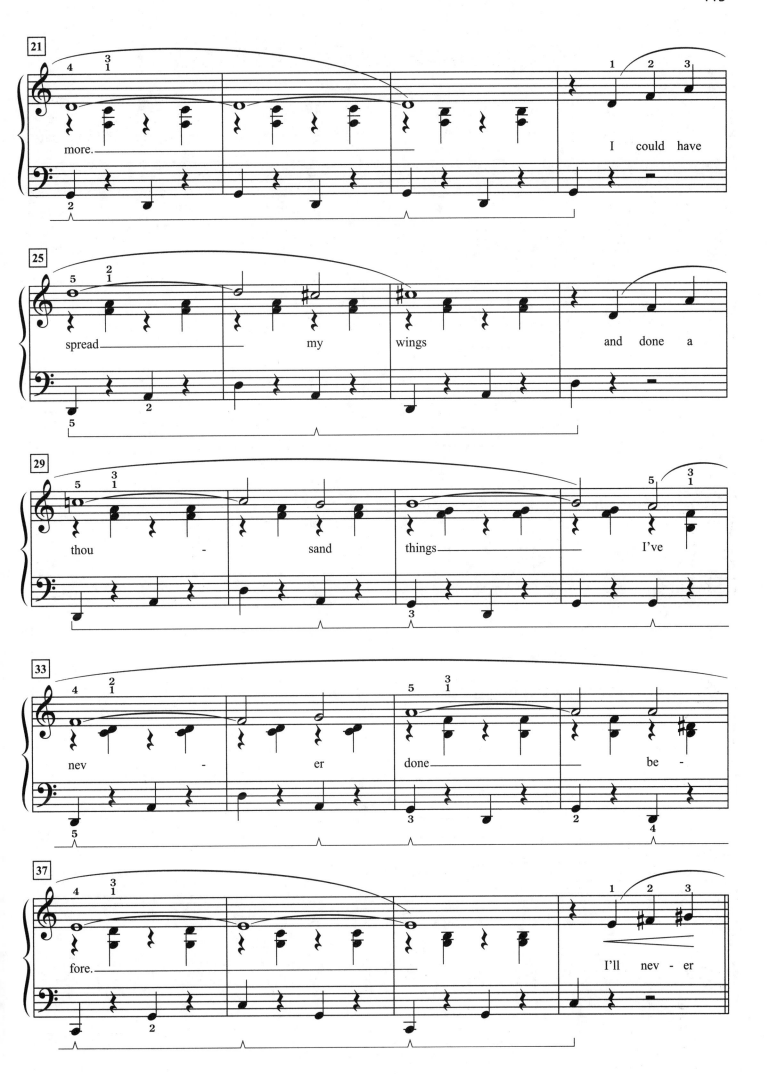

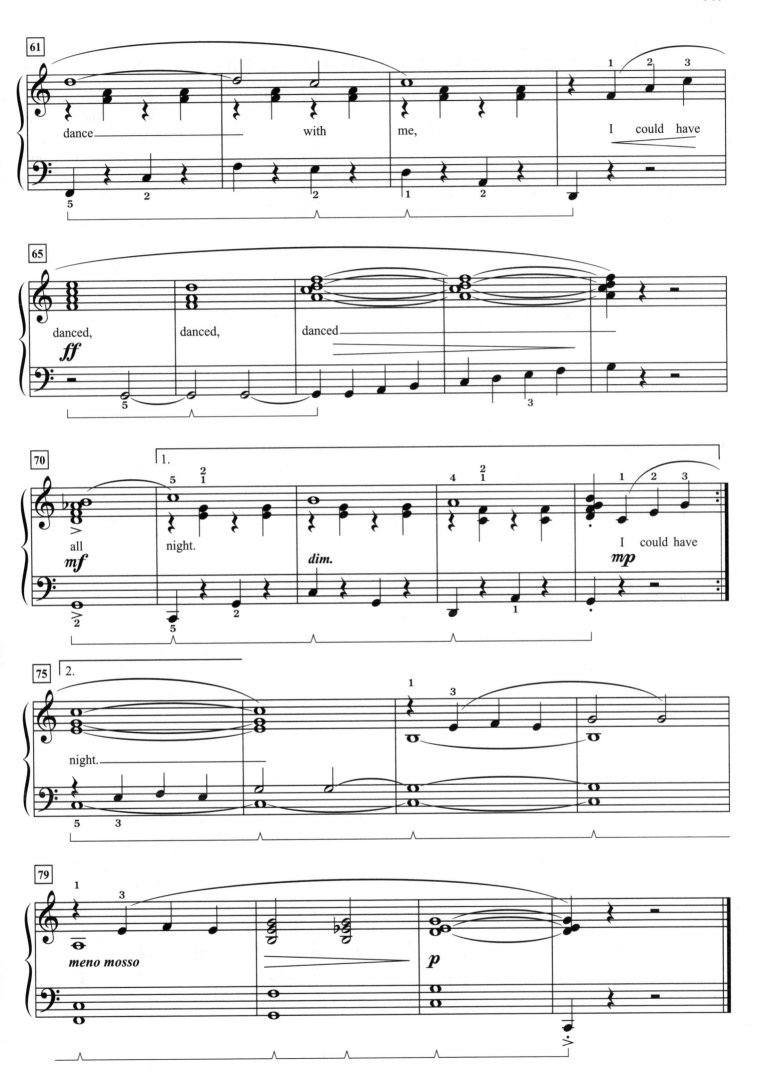

I've Grown Accustomed to Her Face

Lyrics by Alan Jay Lerner
Music by Frederick Loewe
Arranged by Dan Coates

na-ture to me now; like breath-ing out and breath-ing in. I was se-
na-ture to me now; like breath-ing out and breath-ing in. I'm ver-y

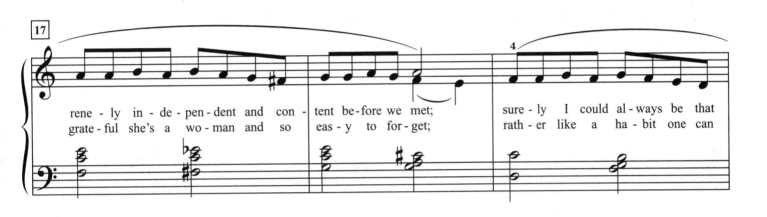

rene - ly in - de - pen-dent and con - tent be-fore we met; sure - ly I could al - ways be that
grate-ful she's a wo-man and so eas - y to for-get; rath - er like a ha - bit one can

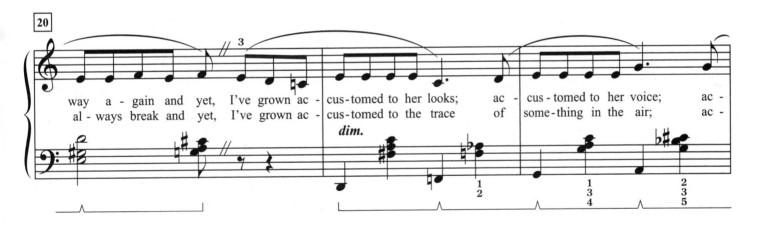

way a - gain and yet, I've grown ac - cus-tomed to her looks; ac - cus-tomed to her voice; ac -
al - ways break and yet, I've grown ac - cus-tomed to the trace of some-thing in the air; ac -

cus - tomed to her face. I've grown ac - face.
cus - tomed to her

On the Street Where You Live

Lyrics by Alan Jay Lerner
Music by Frederick Loewe
Arranged by Dan Coates

122

With a Little Bit of Luck

Lyrics by Alan Jay Lerner
Music by Frederick Loewe
Arranged by Dan Coates

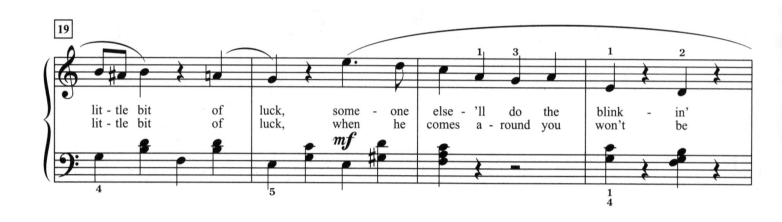

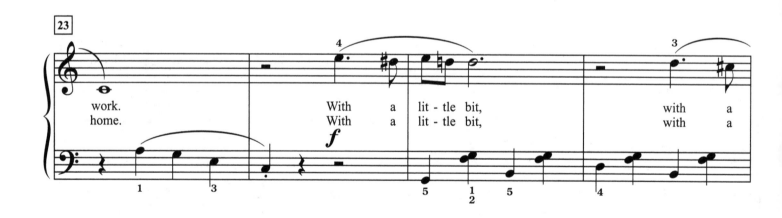

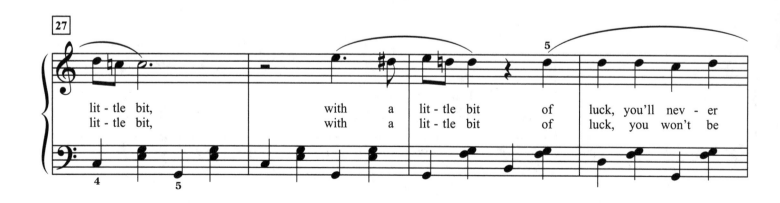

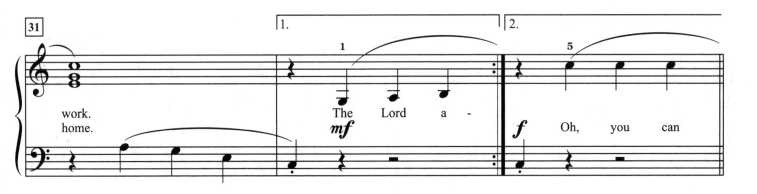

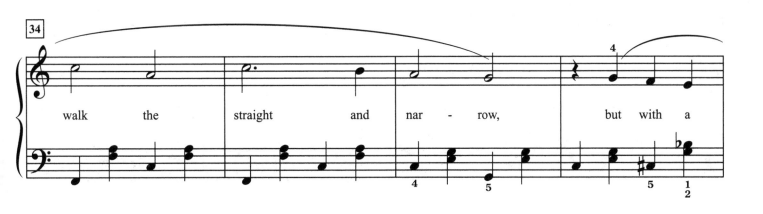

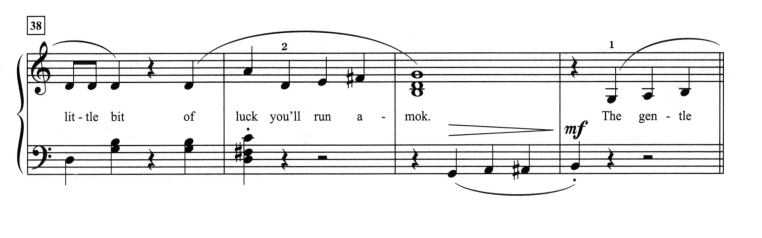

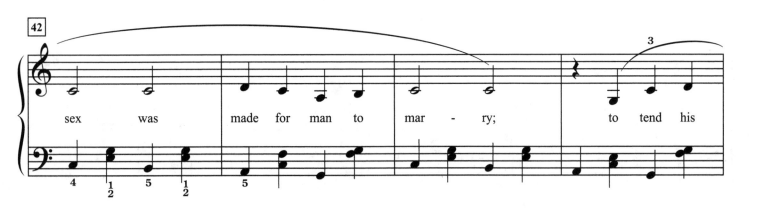

needs and see his food is cooked. The gen - tle

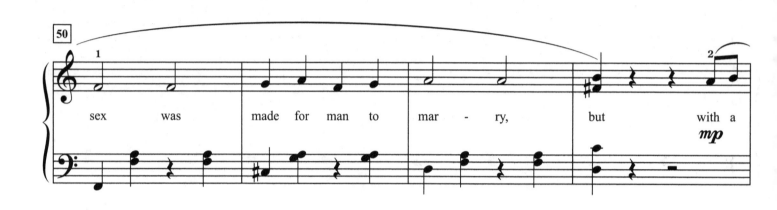

sex was made for man to mar - ry, but with a

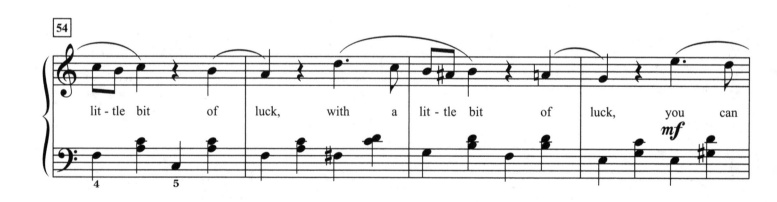

lit - tle bit of luck, with a lit - tle bit of luck, you can

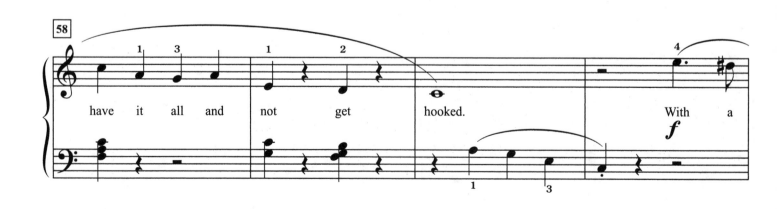

have it all and not get hooked. With a

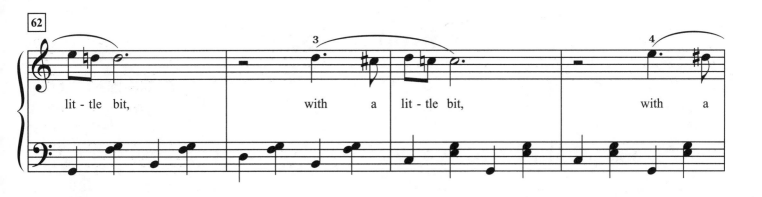

lit - tle bit, with a lit - tle bit, with a

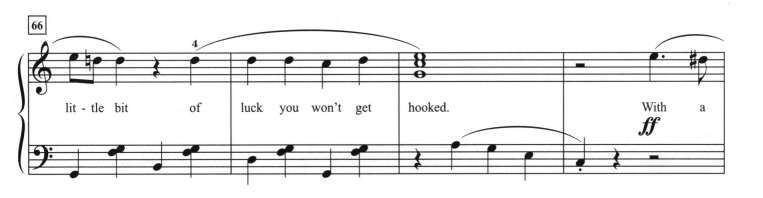

lit - tle bit of luck you won't get hooked. With a

ff

lit - tle bit, with a lit - tle bit, with a

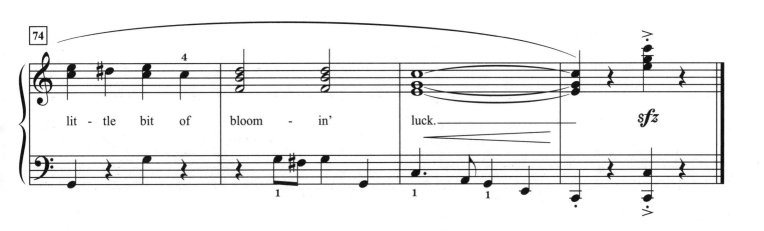

lit - tle bit of bloom - in' luck. _____

sfz

The Rain in Spain

Lyrics by Alan Jay Lerner
Music by Frederick Loewe
Arranged by Dan Coates

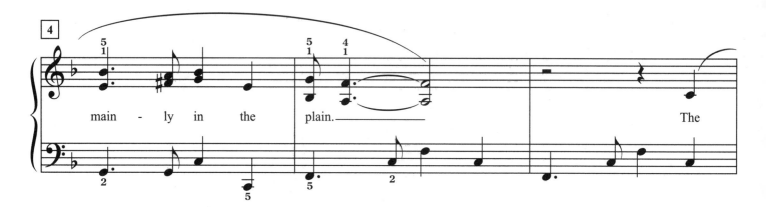

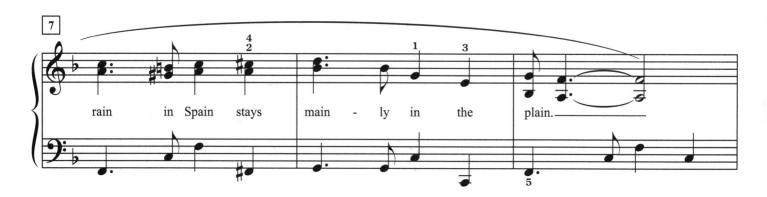

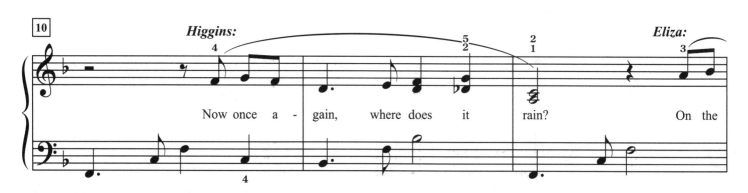

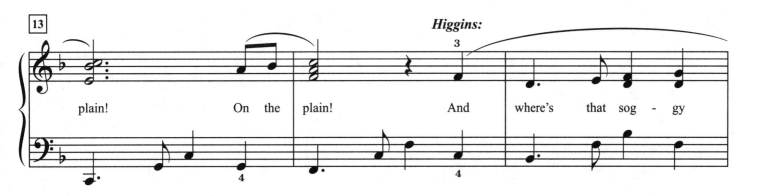

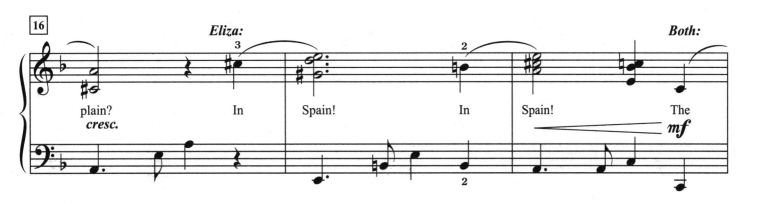

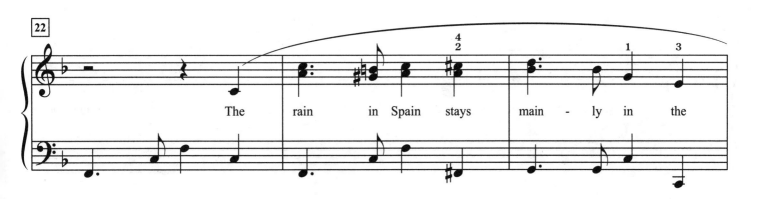

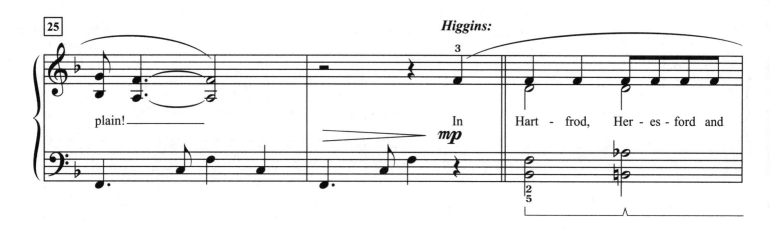

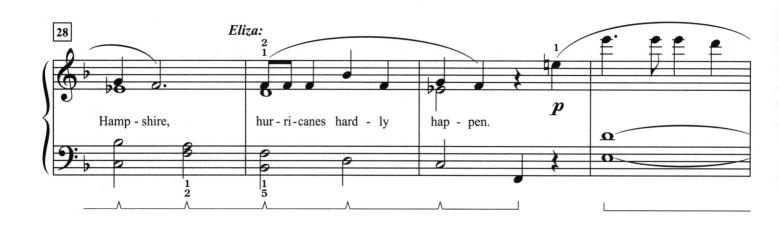

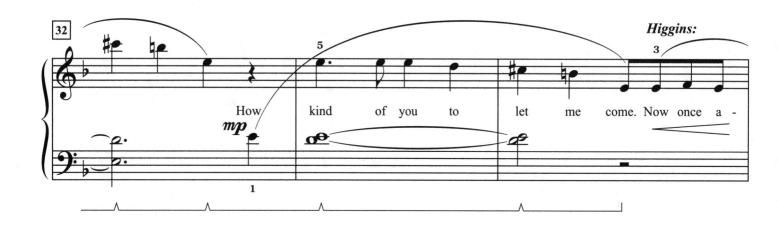

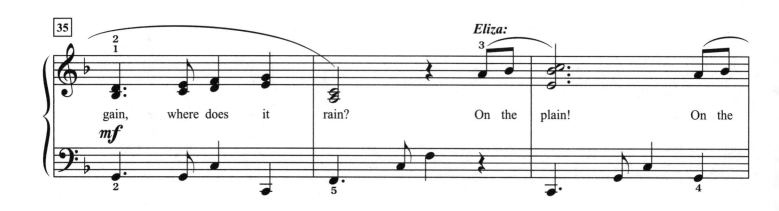

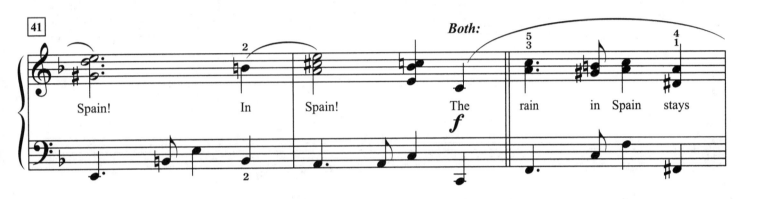

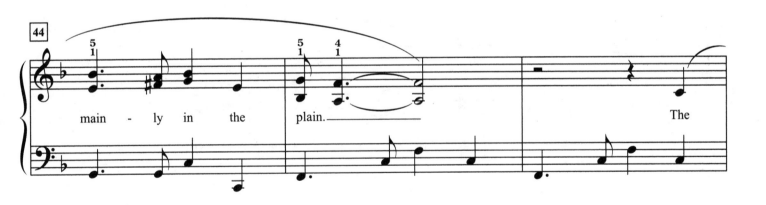

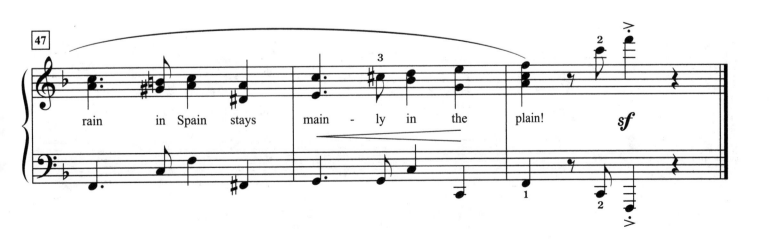

Wouldn't It Be Loverly

Lyrics by Alan Jay Lerner
Music by Frederick Loewe
Arranged by Dan Coates

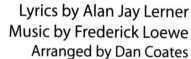

warm face, warm hands, warm feet, oh, would - n't it be

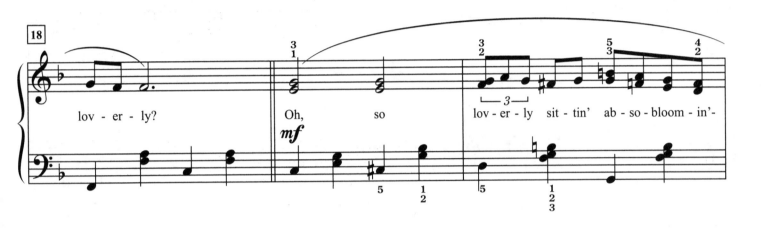

lov - er - ly? Oh, so lov - er - ly sit - tin' ab - so - bloom - in'-

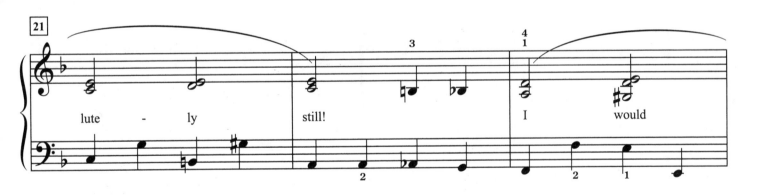

lute - ly still! I would

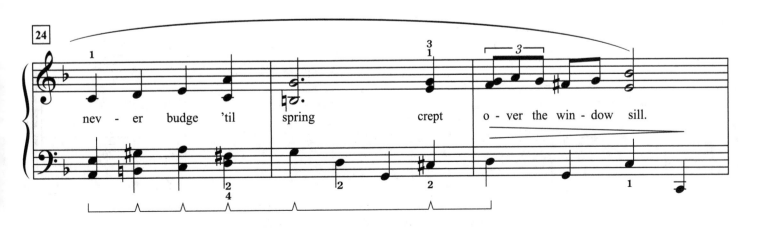

nev - er budge 'til spring crept o - ver the win - dow sill.

Some-one's head rest-in' on my knee, warm and ten - der as he can be;

who takes good care of me. Oh, would - n't it be

lov - er - ly? lov - er - ly? Lov - er - ly!

Lov - er - ly! Lov - er - ly! Lov - er - ly!

rit. e dim.

Bess, You Is My Woman Now

Music and Lyrics by George Gershwin,
Du Bose and Dorothy Heyward and Ira Gershwin
Arranged by Dan Coates

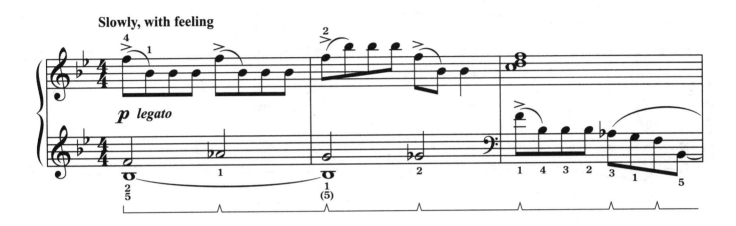

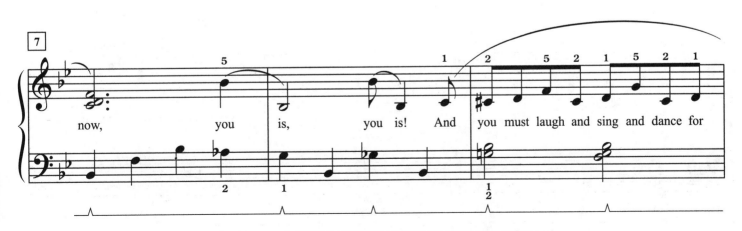

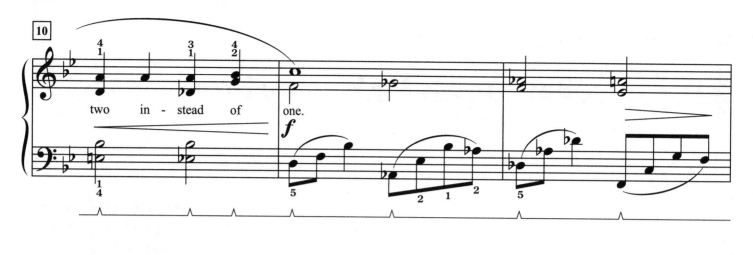

two in - stead of one.

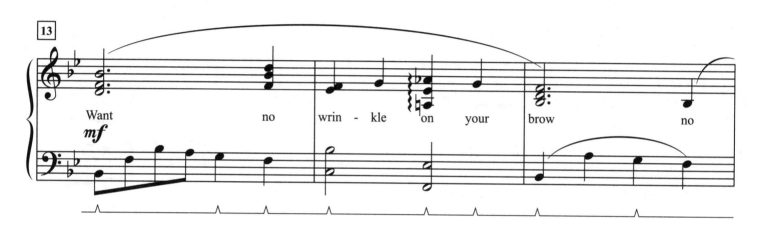

Want no wrin - kle on your brow no

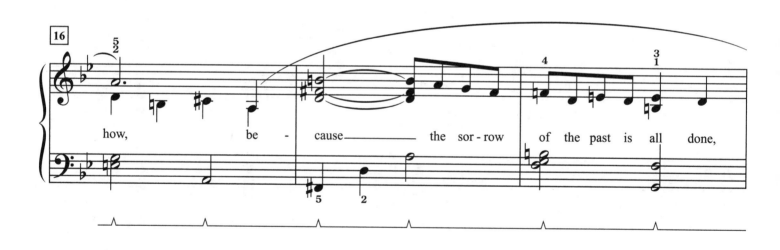

how, be - cause the sor - row of the past is all done,

done. Oh, Bess, my Bess! The real

hap - pi - ness is just be - gun.

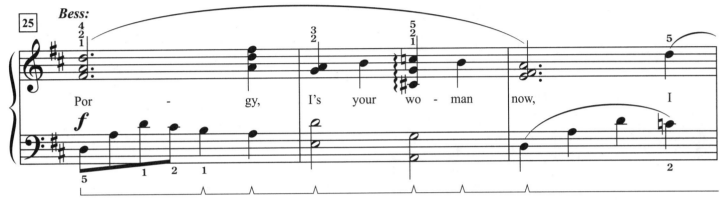

Bess:

Por - gy, I's your wo - man now, I

is, I is! And I ain't nev - er go - in' no - where, 'less you shares the

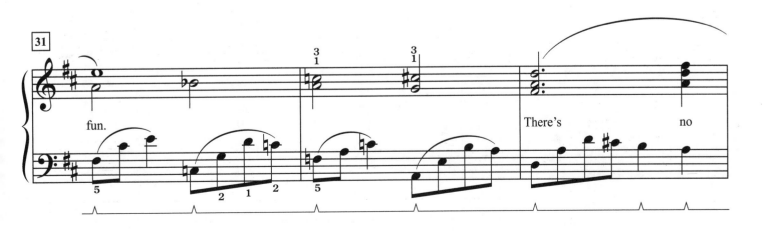

fun. There's no

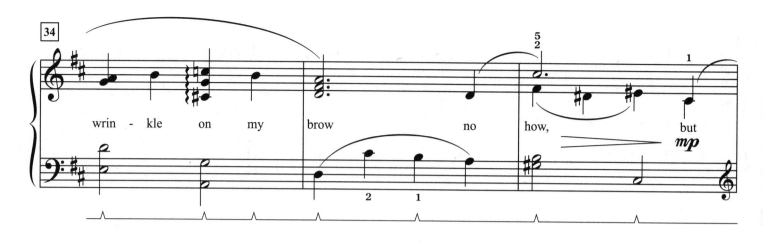

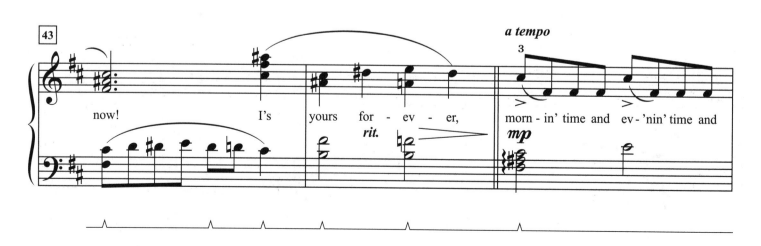

Summertime

Music and Lyrics by George Gershwin,
Du Bose and Dorothy Heyward and Ira Gershwin
Arranged by Dan Coates

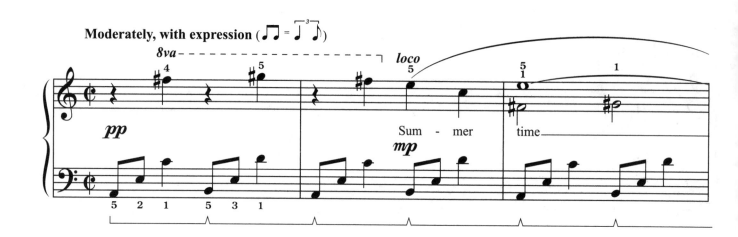

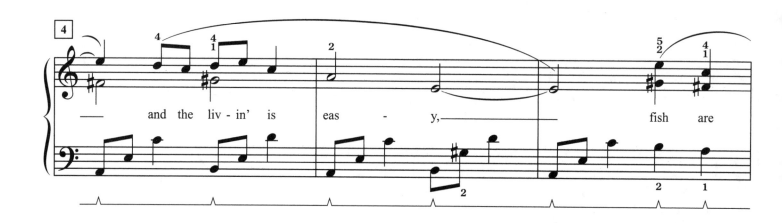

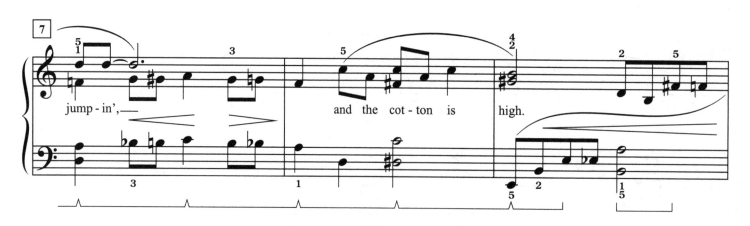

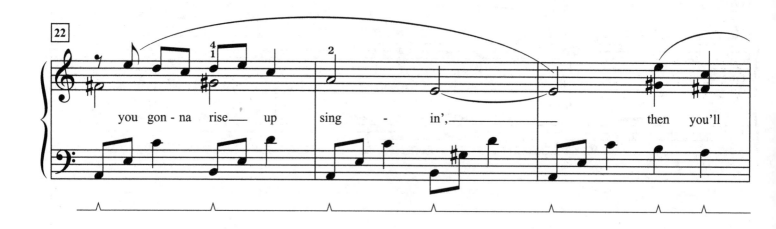

you gon - na rise— up sing - in',_____ then you'll

spread your wings and you'll take to the sky.

But till that morn - in'_____ there's a noth - in' can

harm you, with Dad - dy and Mam - my

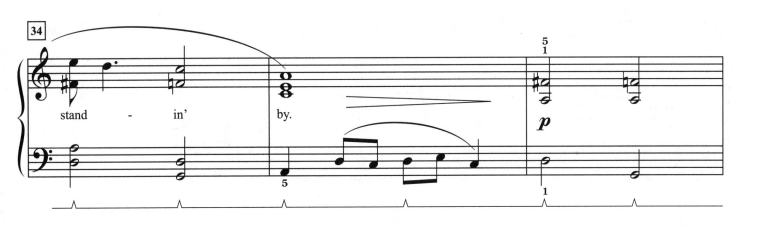

stand - in' by.

p

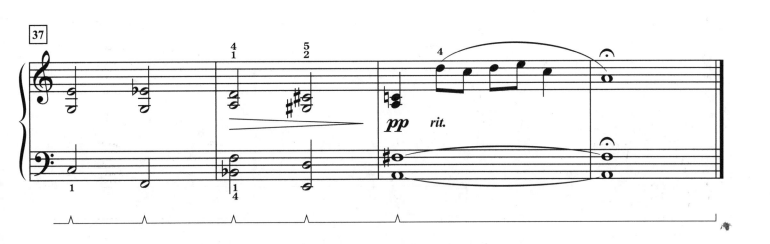

pp *rit.*

It Ain't Necessarily So

Music and Lyrics by George Gershwin,
Du Bose and Dorothy Heyward and Ira Gershwin
Arranged by Dan Coates

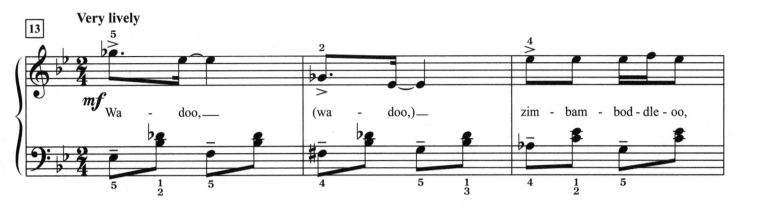

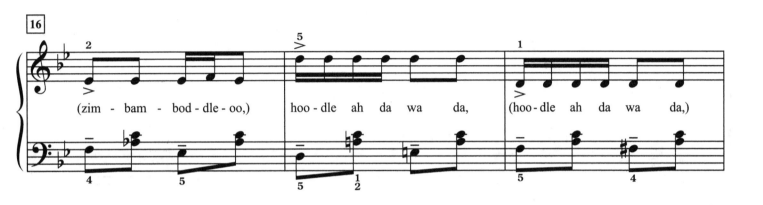

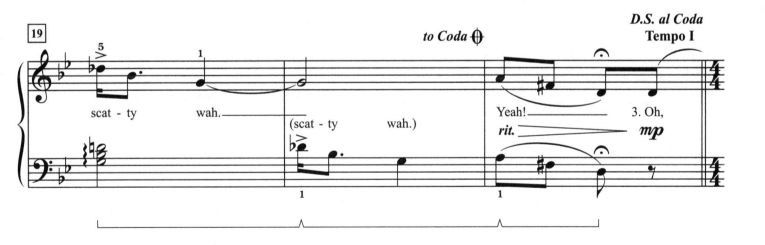

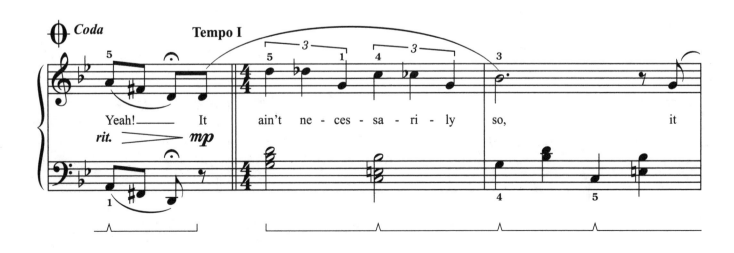

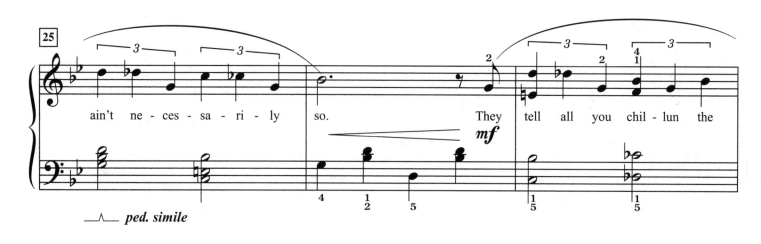

ain't ne - ces - sa - ri - ly so. They tell all you chil - lun the

ped. simile

dev - il's a vil - lian, but t'ain't ne - ces - sa - ri - ly so. To

get in - to hea - ven, don't snap for a sev - en! Live clean! Don't have no

fault. Oh, I takes that gos - pel when - ev - er it's pos' - ble, but

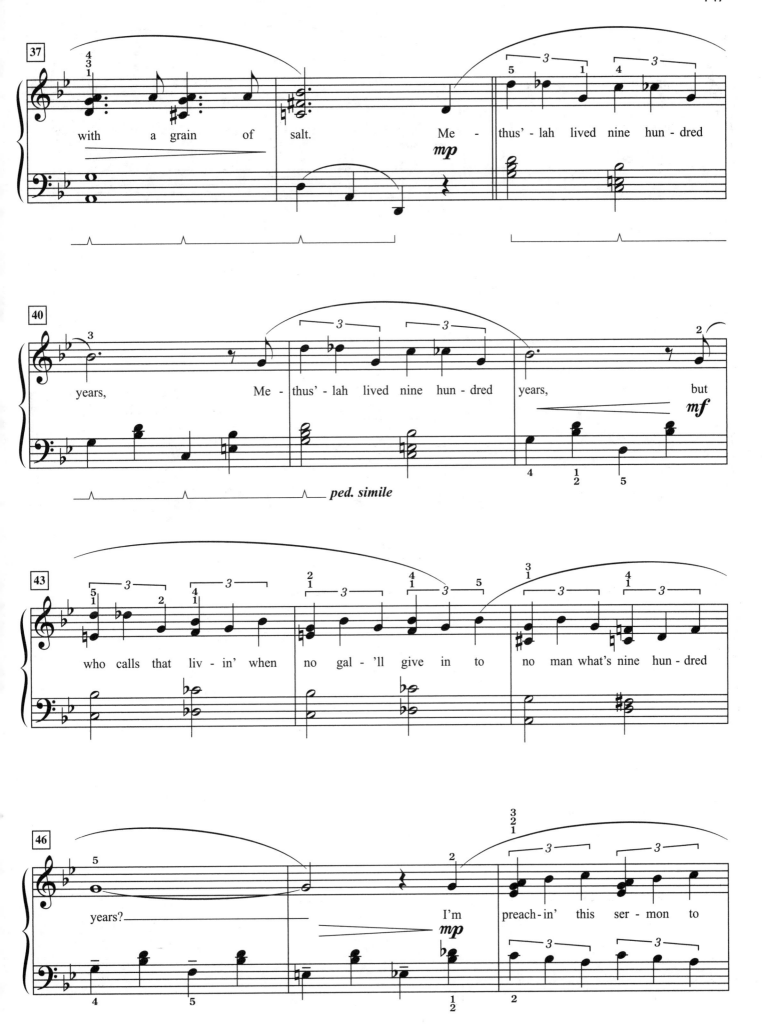

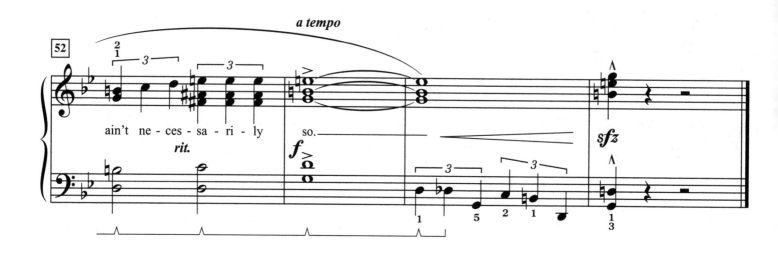

Verse 3:
Oh, Jonah, he lived in the whale,
Oh, Jonah, he lived in the whale,
For he made his home in
That fish's abdomen.
Oh, Jonah, he lived in the whale.

Verse 4:
Li'l Moses was found in a stream,
Li'l Moses was found in a stream,
He floated in water
Till Ole Pharaoh's daughter
She fished him, she says, from that stream.

Make Them Hear You

Lyrics by Lynn Ahrens
Music by Stephen Flaherty
Arranged by Dan Coates

Goodbye, My Love

Lyrics by Lynn Ahrens
Music by Stephen Flaherty
Arranged by Dan Coates

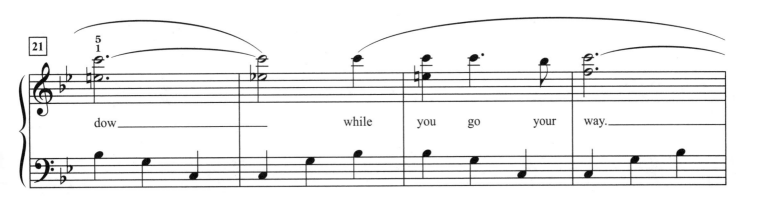

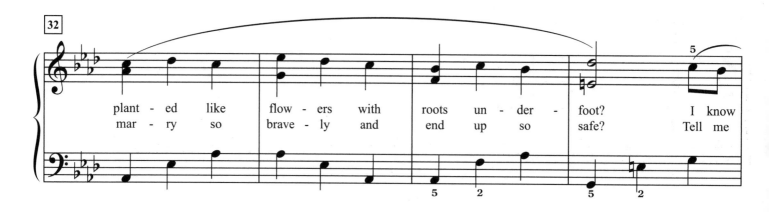

planted like flowers with roots under foot? I know
marry so bravely and end up so safe? Tell me

some of those people have hearts that would rather go
how to be someone whose heart can ex - plore while still

jour - ney - ing on the sea. Tell me,

poco rall.

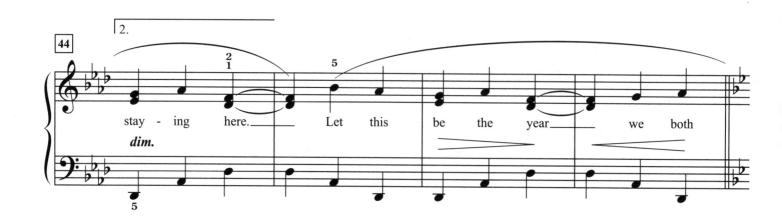

stay - ing here. Let this be the year we both

dim.

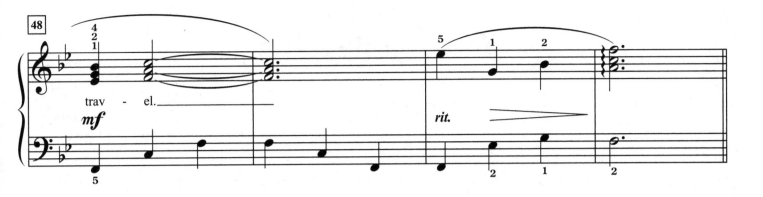

trav - el._____

mf

rit.

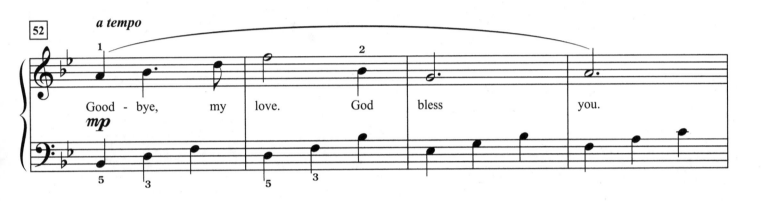

a tempo

Good - bye, my love. God bless you.

mp

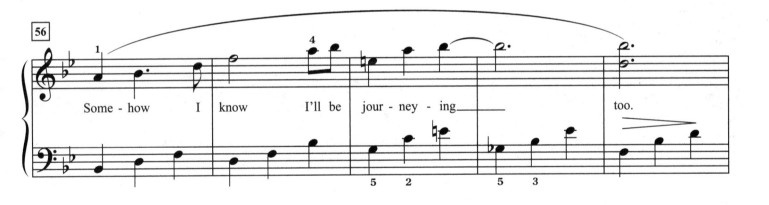

Some - how I know I'll be jour - ney - ing_____ too.

p

rit.

pp

Your Daddy's Son

Lyrics by Lynn Ahrens
Music by Stephen Flaherty
Arranged by Dan Coates

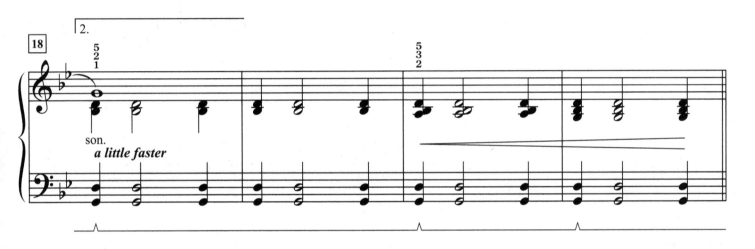

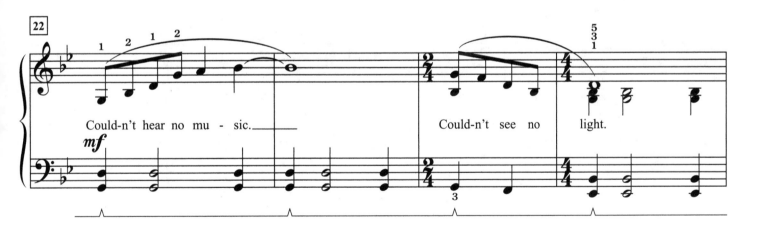

Tears with-out no com - fort, screams with-out no sound.

cresc.

On - ly dark-ness and pain, the an - ger and pain, the blood and the pain! I

f

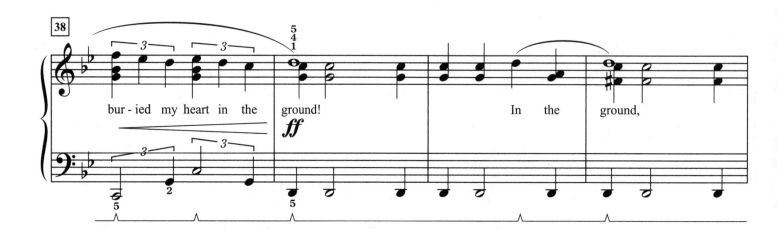

bur - ied my heart in the ground! In the ground,

ff

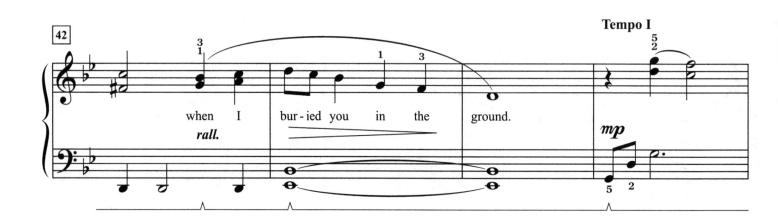

Tempo I

when I bur - ied you in the ground.

rall.

mp

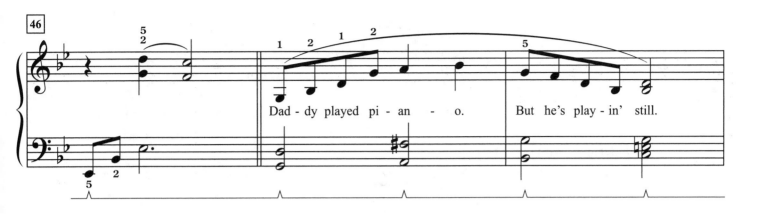

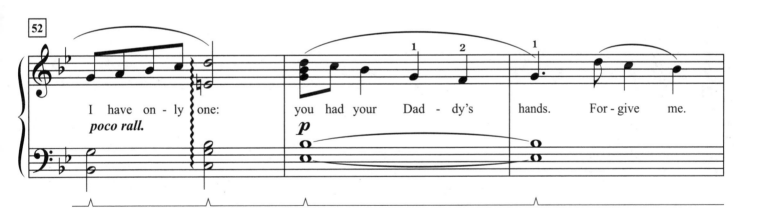

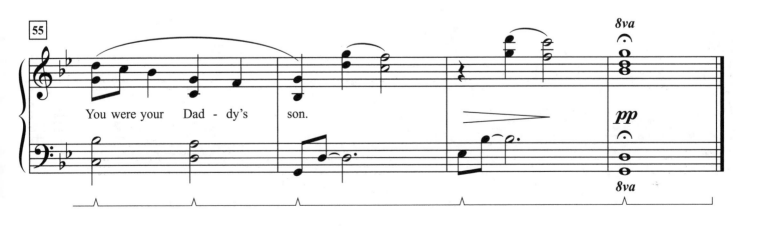

Lily's Eyes

Lyrics by Marsha Norman
Music by Lucy Simon
Arranged by Dan Coates

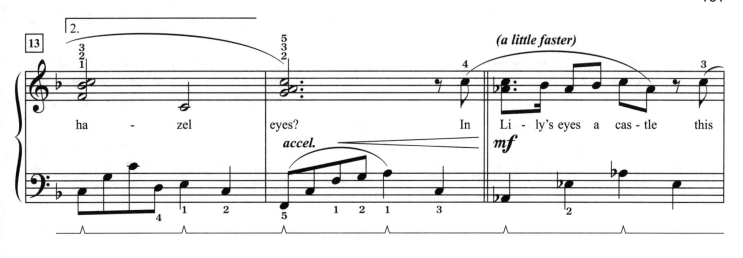

ha - zel eyes? In Li - ly's eyes a cas - tle this

house seemed to be. And I her brav - est knight be - came, my la - dy fair was

Tempo I *(angrily)*
Dr. Craven:

she. She has her eyes, she has my

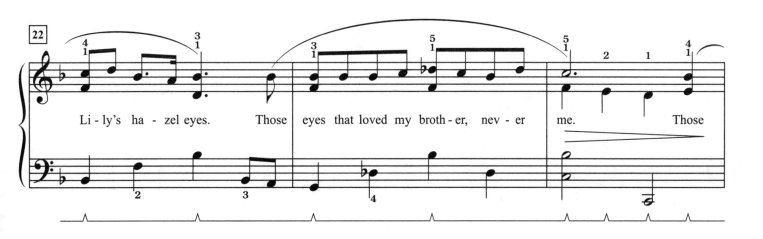

Li - ly's ha - zel eyes. Those eyes that loved my broth - er, nev - er me. Those

eyes that nev - er saw me, nev - er knew I longed to hold her close, to live at last in

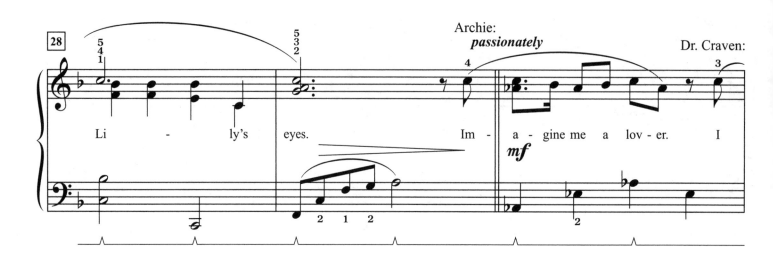

Li - ly's eyes.   Archie: *passionately*   Im - a - gine me a lov - er.   Dr. Craven: I

longed for the day she'd turn and see me stand - ing there. Would   Both: God had let her

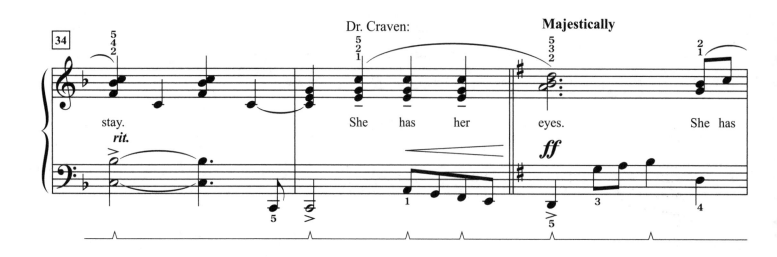

stay.   Dr. Craven: She has her   **Majestically** eyes.   She has

How Could I Ever Know?

Lyrics by Marsha Norman
Music by Lucy Simon
Arranged by Dan Coates

All for You

Lyrics by Lynn Ahrens
Music by Stephen Flaherty
Arranged by Matt Hyzer

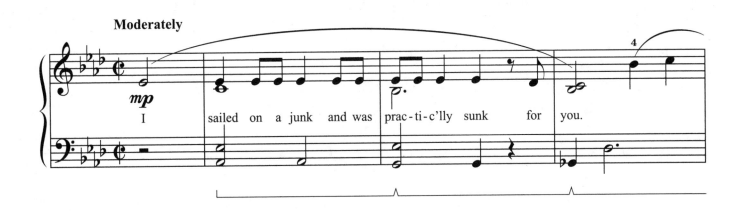

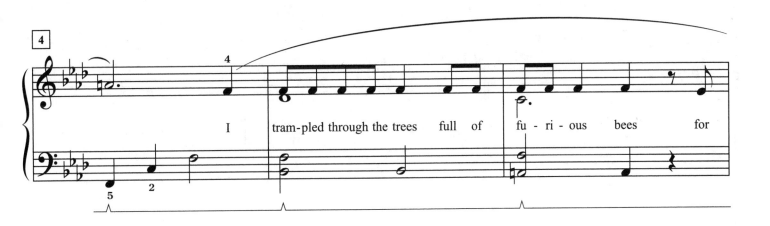

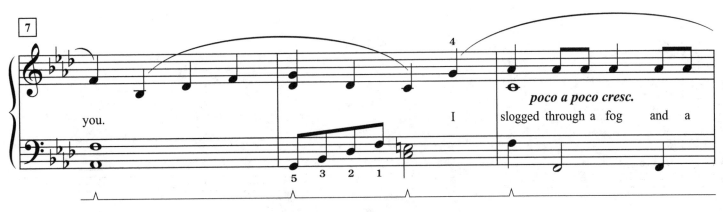

168

choking smog, down a soggy slope through a stinking bog, while my

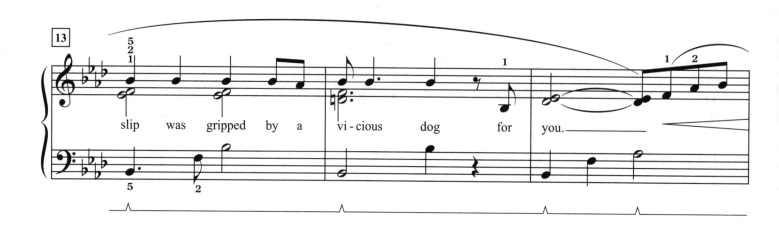

slip was gripped by a vicious dog for you._____

I gal-loped through the snow in e-le-ven be-low_____ for

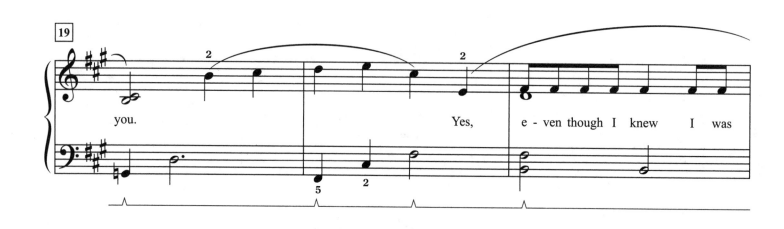

you. Yes, e-ven though I knew I was

you!_____ There's noth-ing that I would-n't and I

couldn-n't and I have-n't gone through!... rit. I

Deliberately (a bit slower)

sprained my lit-tle toe, but I hob-bled like so for you.

Then came the hit and run, but I stag-gered on one for

you._____ Now here I am, the

worse for wear, and here you are. I'm here! You're there! And

may - be NOW you'll know I care for you! *sub.* ***p*** It

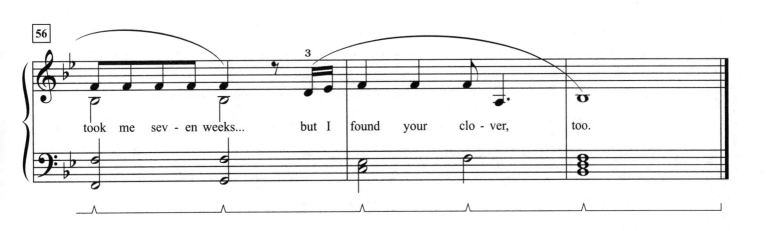

took me sev - en weeks... but I found your clo - ver, too.

Alone in the Universe

Lyrics by Lynn Ahrens
Music by Stephen Flaherty
Arranged by Matt Hyzer

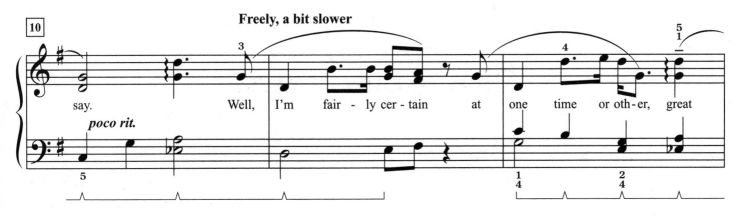

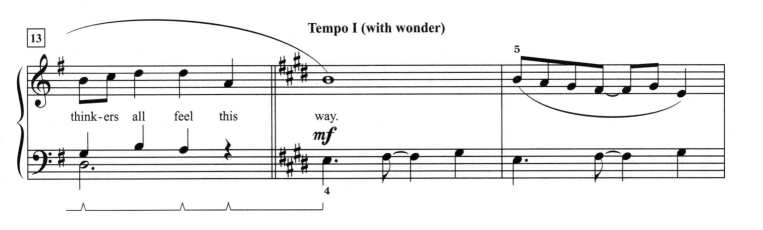

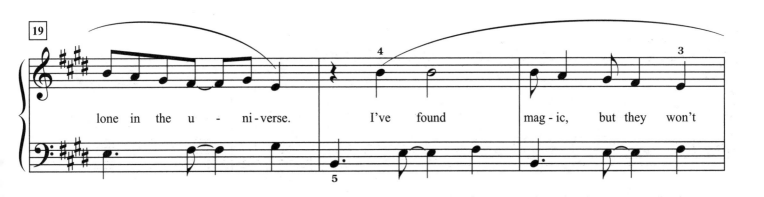

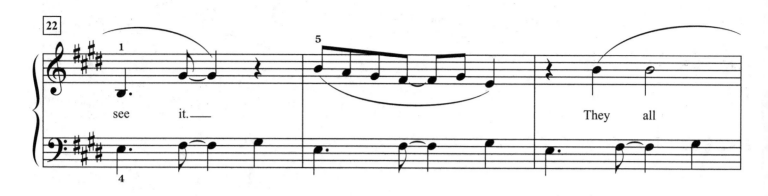

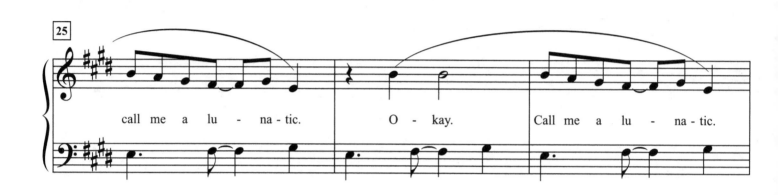

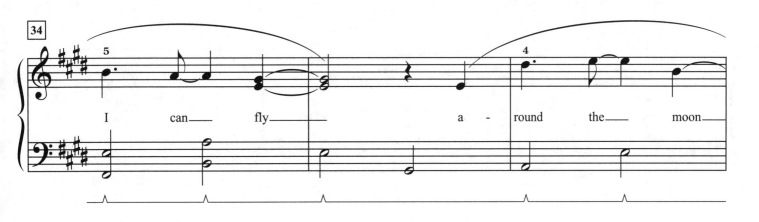

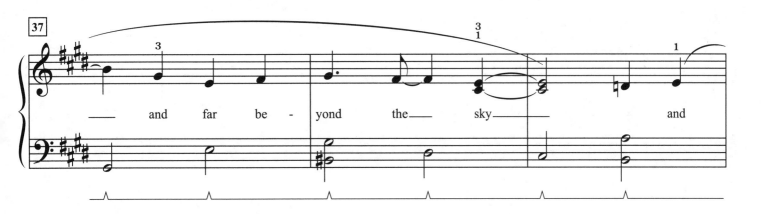

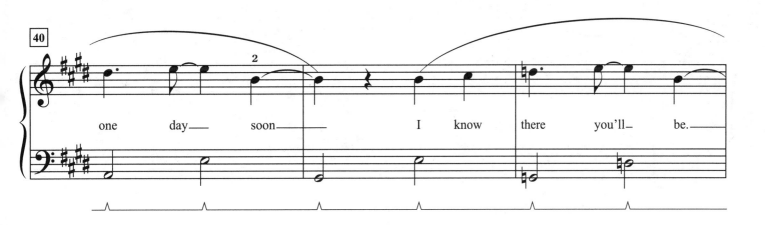

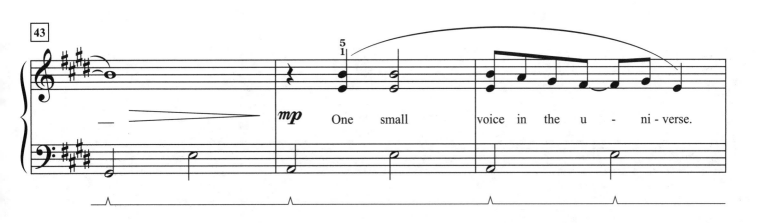

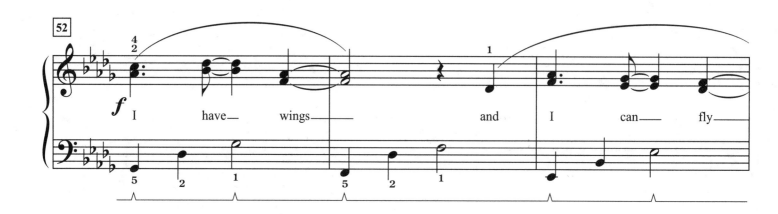

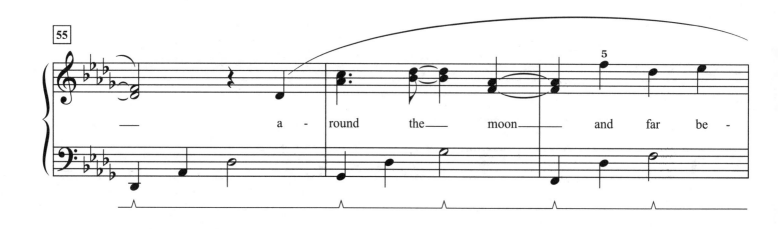

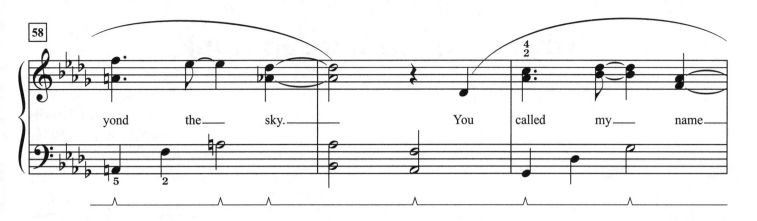

yond the___ sky.___ You called my___ name___

___ and you set me___ free... *mp* One small

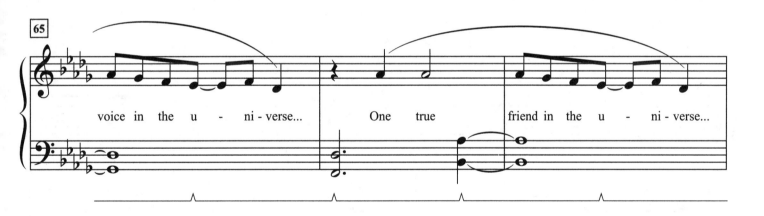

voice in the u - ni - verse... One true friend in the u - ni - verse...

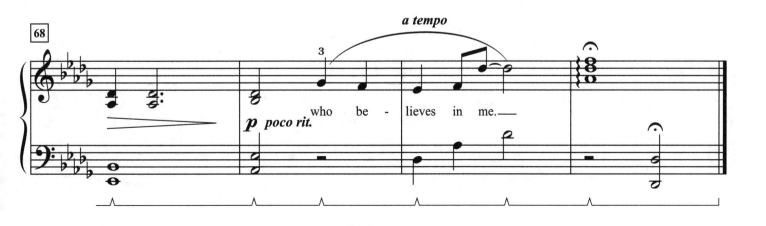

who be - lieves in me.___

Oh, the Thinks You Can Think

Lyrics by Lynn Ahrens
Music by Stephen Flaherty
Arranged by Matt Hyzer

lin - ing up   to   get   loose…   Oh, the Thinks you can think

when you think a - bout   Seuss!

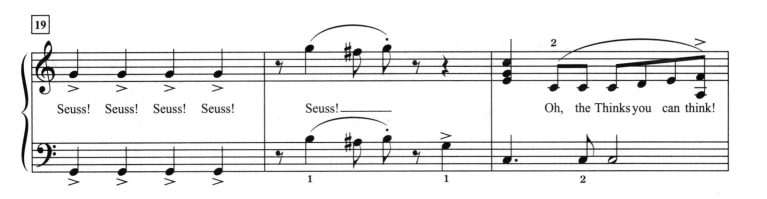

Seuss! Seuss! Seuss! Seuss!   Seuss!   Oh, the Thinks you can think!

Think and won - der and dream   far and wide as you dare.   Oh, the Thinks you can think!

When your Thinks have run dry   in the blink of an eye   there's an - oth - er Think

there.   If you o - pen your mind,   oh, the Thinks you will find

lin - ing up to get loose.   Oh, the Thinks you can think!

Oh, the Thinks you can think!   Oh, the Thinks you can think!   Oh, the Thinks you can

Biggest Blame Fool

Lyrics by Lynn Ahrens
Music by Stephen Flaherty
Arranged by Matt Hyzer

Not While I'm Around

Music and Lyrics by
Stephen Sondheim
Arranged by Kathryn Lounsbery

now - a - days. I'll send 'em howl - ing, I don't care,

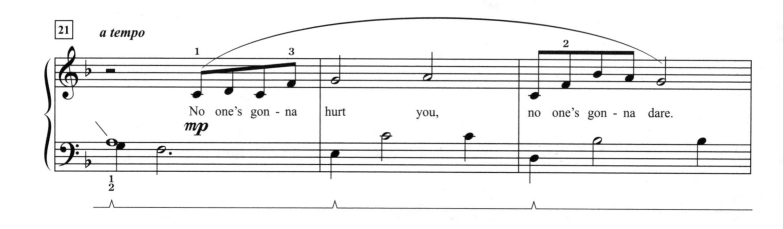

I got ways.

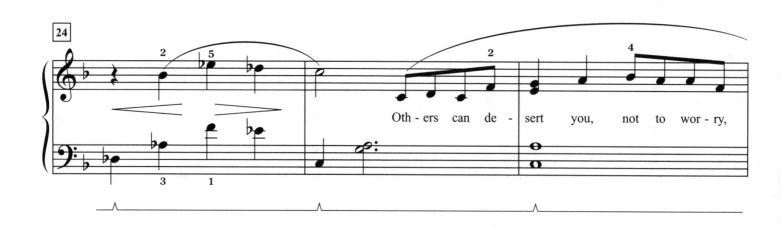

No one's gon - na hurt you, no one's gon - na dare.

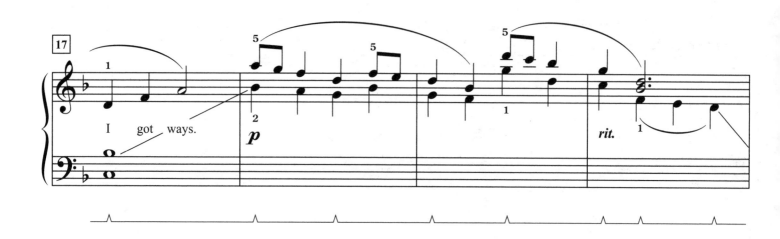

Oth - ers can de - sert you, not to wor - ry,

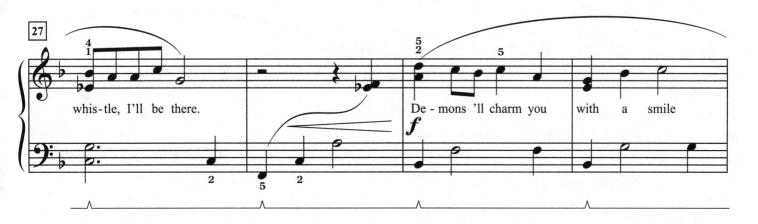

whis-tle, I'll be there. De - mons 'll charm you with a smile

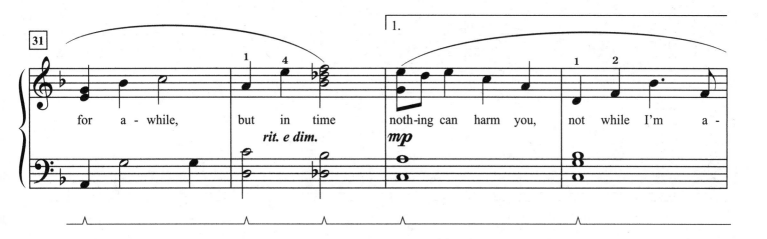

for a - while, but in time noth-ing can harm you, not while I'm a-

rit. e dim.

1.

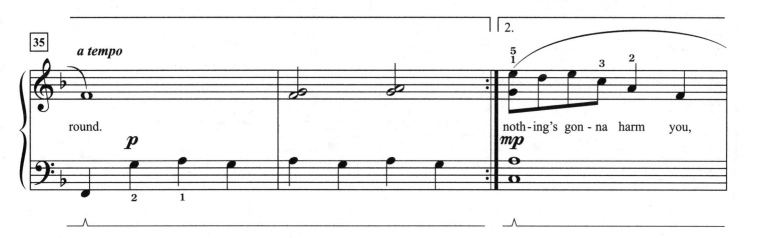

a tempo

round. noth-ing's gon - na harm you,

2.

not while I'm a - round. *rit. e dim.*

Johanna

Music and Lyrics by
Stephen Sondheim
Arranged by Kathryn Lounsbery

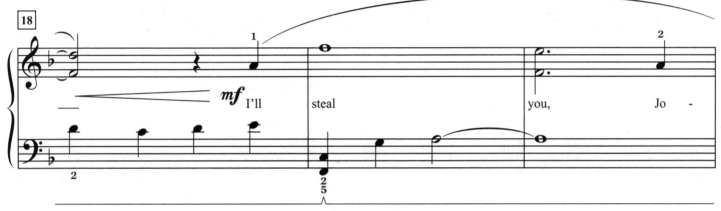

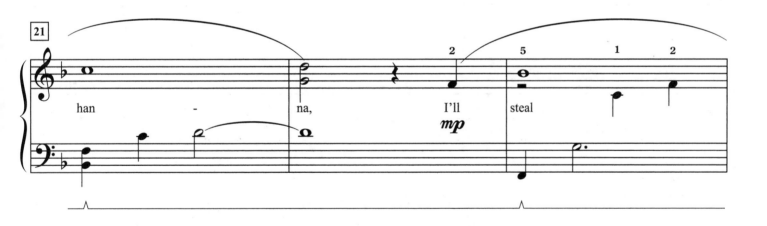

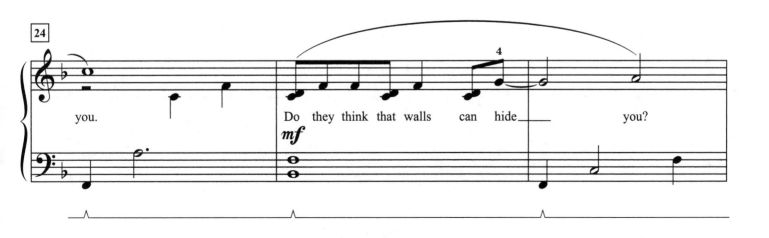

E - ven now I'm at your win - dow. I am in the dark be - side

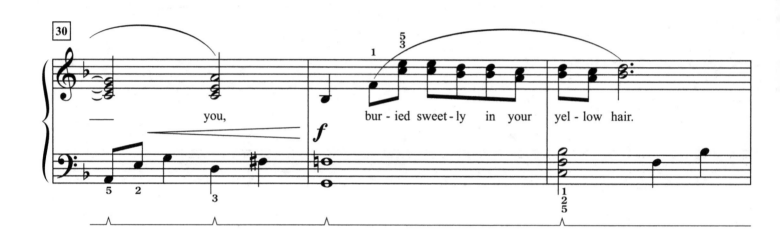

you, bur - ied sweet - ly in your yel - low hair.

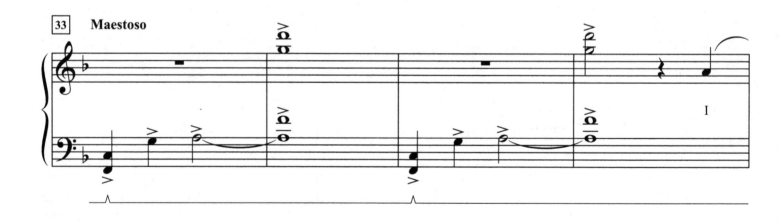

Maestoso

I

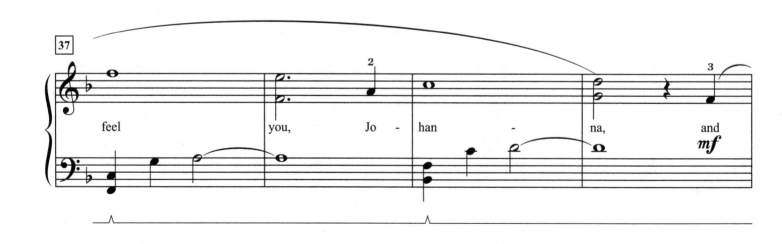

feel you, Jo - han - na, and

one day I'll steal you.

cresc. Till I'm with you then I'm with you there, sweet-ly bur-ied in your

yel-low hair.

Pretty Women

Music and Lyrics by
Stephen Sondheim
Arranged by Kathryn Lounsbery

stand-ing on the__ stair, some-thing in them__

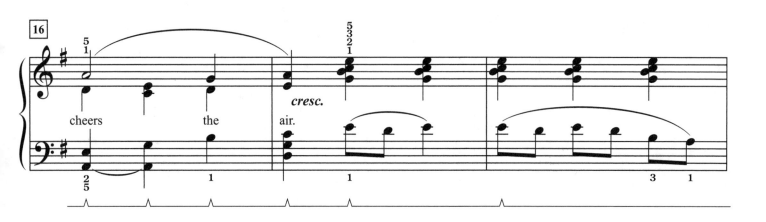

cheers the air. *cresc.*

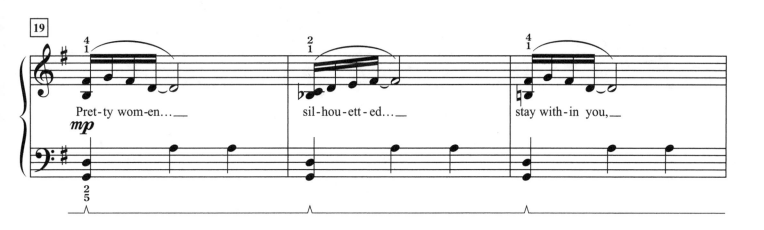

Pret-ty wom-en...__ sil-hou-ett-ed...__ stay with-in you,__

mp

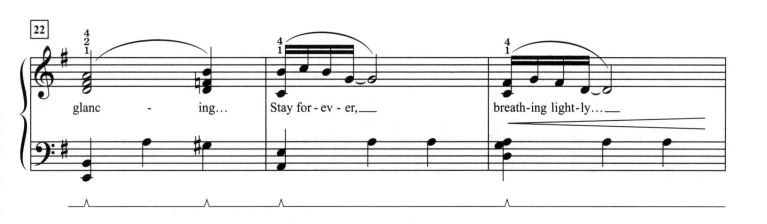

glanc - ing... Stay for - ev - er,__ breath-ing light-ly...__

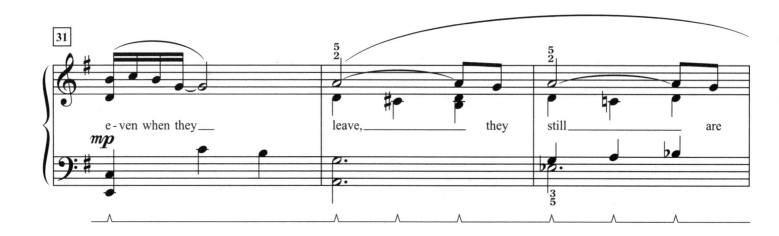

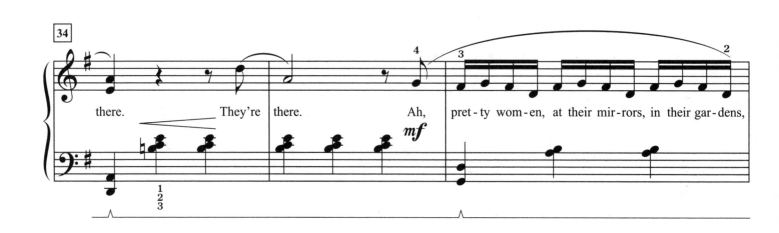

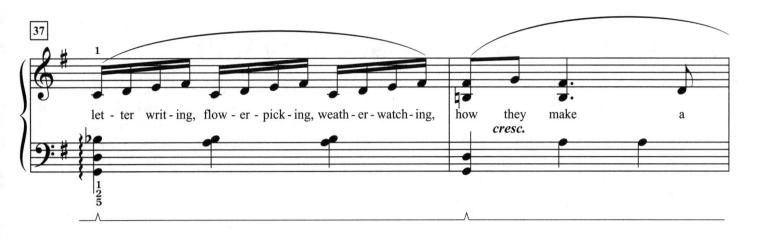

let - ter writ - ing, flow - er - pick - ing, weath - er - watch - ing, how they make a

man sing! Proof of heav - en__ as you're liv - ing,__

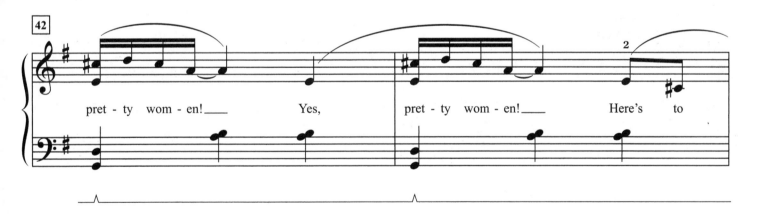

pret - ty wom - en!__ Yes, pret - ty wom - en!__ Here's to

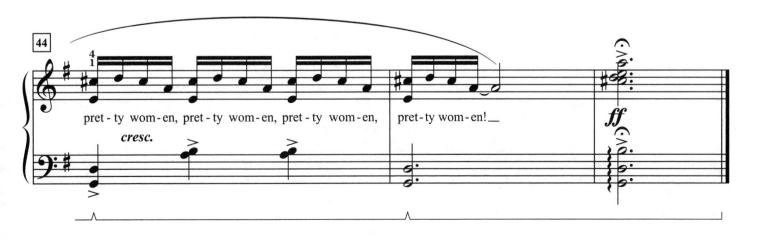

pret - ty wom - en, pret - ty wom - en, pret - ty wom - en, pret - ty wom - en!__

The Ballad of Sweeney Todd

Music and Lyrics by
Stephen Sondheim
Arranged by Kathryn Lounsbery

Mysteriously, with motion

At-tend the tale of Swee-ney Todd. His skin was pale and his eye was odd. He shaved the fa-ces of gen-tle-men who nev-er there-af-ter were heard of a-gain.

By the Sea

Music and Lyrics by
Stephen Sondheim
Arranged by Kathryn Lounsbery

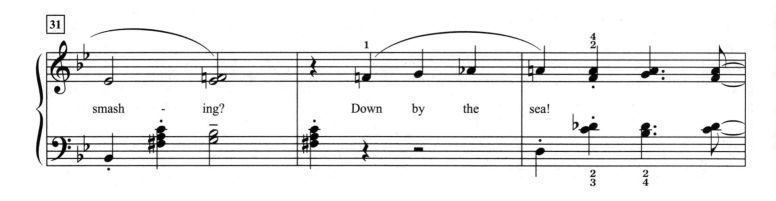

smash - ing? Down by the sea!

I can

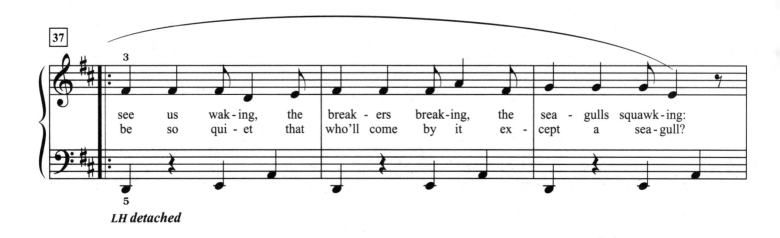

see us wak-ing, the break-ers break-ing, the sea - gulls squawk-ing:
be so qui - et that who'll come by it ex - cept a sea-gull?

LH detached

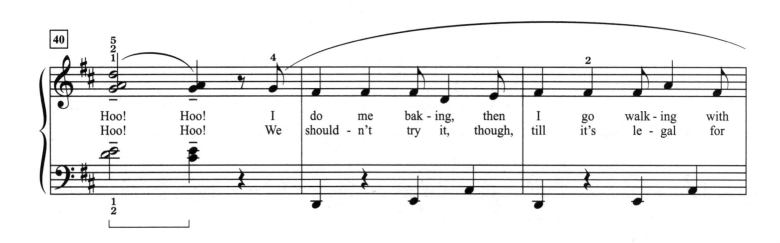

Hoo! Hoo! I do me bak-ing, then I go walk-ing with
Hoo! Hoo! We should - n't try it, though, till it's le - gal for

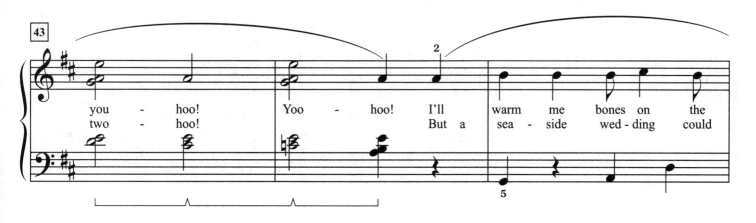

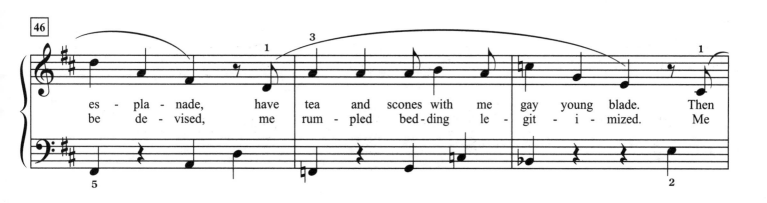

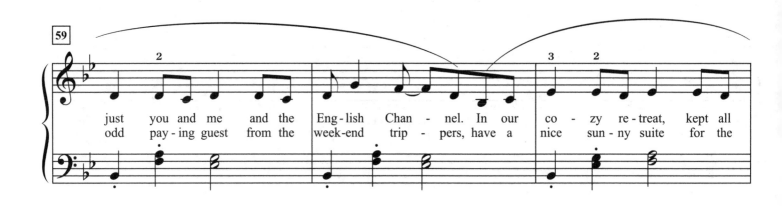

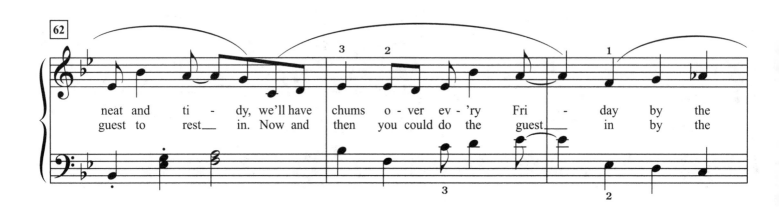

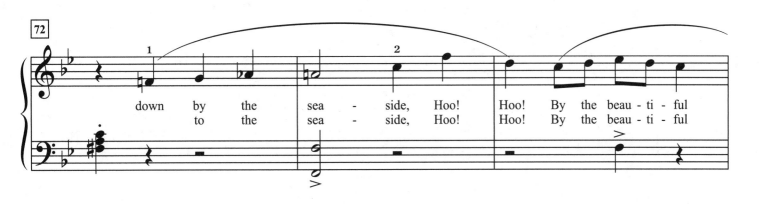

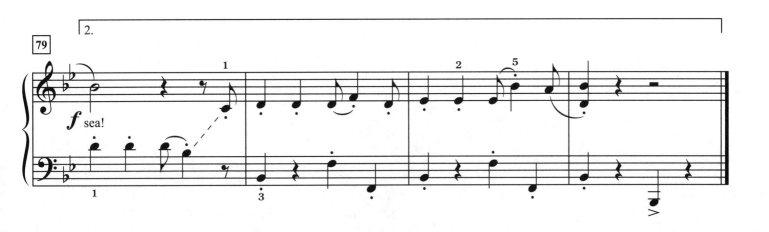